HOT CHICKS WITH DOUCHEBAGS

HOT CHICKS
WITH
DOUCHEBAGS

Exploring the Hottie/Scrotey Phenomenon

Jay Louis

SIMON SPOTLIGHT ...on • Toronto • Sydney

SIMON SPOTLIGHT ENTERTAINMENT
A Division of Simon & Schuster, Inc.
1230 Avenue of the Americas
New York, NY 10020

First Simon Spotlight Entertainment trade paperback edition July 2008

SIMON SPOTLIGHT ENTERTAINMENT and colophon are trademarks
of Simon & Schuster, Inc.

For information about special discounts for bulk purchases,
please contact Simon & Schuster Special Sales at 1-800-456-6798
or business@simonandschuster.com.

Designed by Dana Sloan

Manufactured in the United States of America

10 9 8 7 6 5 4 3 2

Library of Congress Cataloging-in-Publication Data is available.

ISBN-13: 978-1-4169-5788-1
ISBN-10:   1-4169-5788-X

For my mother, Barbara, and my father, Larry, who taught me how to laugh at *The 'Bag Within* all of us.

And for douchebags everywhere. You people need a smack.

Douchebag (doosh-bag) n.

1. A feminine hygiene device used for cleansing.

2. A heterosexual male attempting to attract a female through the use of excessive cosmetic products, hand gestures, fist pumping, loud shirts, upturned collars, jewelry, and intricately carved facial hair. Often found displaying themselves in their natural habitat, clubs, where they attempt to cohabitate with young women while sticking out their tongues and making facial expressions known as the *douche-face*. Alternate forms include *Douche, Douchebaggery, Douchebaguous, Scrotebag, Guido, Choadbag, 'Bag, Babagadouche,* and *Total and Complete Asswipe.*

CONTENTS

BEFORE WE BEGIN, I had to take a moment and show you the Hemorrhoid.

He didn't really fit in with any of the section samples for the book because, well, he's the human form of large, painful, and swollen veins in the rectum. But it is worth it to pause for a moment and simply gaze at this absolutely ridiculous ass-clown. And I mean that literally.

As we will examine in this book, douchebaggery comes in many forms, permutations, variations, and stubbly manifestations. But always present across this spectrum of scrote is a certain core radiating douchosity. A *douche glow*, if you will.

Viewing the Hemorrhoid, we see that glow.

How is it possible that such a skeezed-out ass-pimple can corral two blonde Popsicles?

Answering that question is our mission statement.

And so we begin.

CONFRONTING THE DOUCHEBAG PLAGUE

THEY'RE EVERYWHERE.

Greased-up foreheads. Spiky, frosted cactus hair. Glittering designer dog tags. Giant blinged-out diamond necklaces swinging wildly around their necks as they pump their fists to Euro-trash techno. A societal spew.

These primal, grunting spawns of Satan prowl across our country like a marauding horde of Unholy Douche Crusaders, inhabiting our cities and flooding our suburbs like a rancid plague. They're everywhere: large metropolitan areas, suburban strip malls, even in empty, vacuous wastelands like the Everglades of Florida, or Dallas, Texas.

From sea to douchey sea, ours is a culture overwhelmed by this festering blight, a perfect storm of greased-up bodies, plucked eyebrows, and tight see-through Armani/Exchange T-shirts.

And then there's the other half of the equation. The hotties by their sides, perched on their arms like dazed Serengeti Boobie Parrots. Sweet melon balls of befuddled youth balancing, circus-act-style, on ginormous high heels.

Innocent cuties, lost in the maze of fist-pumping douchewanks, completely oblivious to the hulking half-human monstrosities clutching at their thighs.

How did this happen?

What answers lie beneath this paradox of hottie and douchebag? And how did our society reach this rank state of cultural douche-rot?

These are the questions we are driven to explore.

In this book, we will identify every type of 'bag within the douche spectrum, from the youthful stage-1 Fratbags to the polluted, noxious stage-4 DJ Club Douche. We will tap directly into the core of not only how douchebaggery manifests, but also how it corrupts the hottie within its wily, greased-up charms. These unnatural cohabitations must be exposed to the disinfecting light of detailed scrutiny if we have any hope of societal redress.

We will journey upriver, venturing farther into the dark, swampy gel-infested waters of clubland douchitude than ever before. We will ride on until answers come to us like those early dawn revelations of peyote-inspired Iroquois Indians who asked themselves so long ago, "Why is the White Man so douchey?"

Like hallucinating stigmatic nuns or perplexed Maori studying Aussie Rules Football, we will write our answers in hair gel on the walls of our collective cultural psyche.

Get ready.

Crack open a Red Bull, turn up the bass on the Nelly remix, and prepare yourself for a deep, probing journey inside the wrongness that is the cultural blight known as Hot Chicks with Douchebags.

PART 1

A BRIEF HISTORY
OF DOUCHE

...defines a douchebag? Is it the bling? The face? ...

...ll of those. Yet it is none of those.

...essence, douchebaggery is the performative r...

...cking male in an utterly false, constructed, sm...

...thy way.

...of the 'bag is simple: to dazzle the hottie by di...

...gender inversion of the traditional male-to-fem...

...wank confuses the hottie's frame of reference b...

...alance with sheer spectacle, and thus intrigues...

...ough the performance of masquerade: the fake...

...ved chest, and plucked eyebrows of modern c...

Once achieving this state of hyper-reality, the gelled up über-douche brands his overly quaffed self as a source of value for the female to acquire, like an expensive pair of designer jeans.

Douchitude is the mask. The role.

Anyone can adopt the tropes of douchebaggery, be they white, be they black, be they Asian, Latino, or New Jersey. Like any pure Zen art, douchosity comes from the soul. It is not identified by a 'bag's genetic characteristics or cat-neutering fuglyness, but radiates from his popped collar with the power of a thousand techno-dance remixes.

But this is just a textbook overview.

To truly understand douchebaggery, we must start at the beginning. My beginning. My epiphany. My first moment of realization of the profound wrongness of the plague of hottie/douchebaggery infecting our culture like a mutant herp virus.

My search to explore the outer reaches of cultural 'baggitude, and journey inside myself: to understand *The 'Bag Within*.

My mission to save the hotties. My quest to mock the 'bags. And my spiritual voyage to banish the hottie/douchey plague forever.

Or at least make fun of them in book form.

CHAPTER 1

HOHOS AND NIGHT TRAIN: MY MOMENT OF DOUCHE-CLARITY

To fear douchebaggery, my friends, is only to think ourselves wise, without being wise: for it is to think that we know what we do not know about douchebags.

— SOCRATES

I CAN PINPOINT the exact moment when I realized the profound wrongness of the hottie/douchey plague. It was instantaneous and utterly transforming, like getting smacked in the head with a giant bottle of Grey Goose vodka. Or firing a giant fake diamond earring dipped in Rockstar Energy Drink up my nose with a nail gun.

It all began with my Original Hot Chick.

We all have one. The first. The hottie who tied your guts into Gordian knots and tap-danced on your liver like a ballet-leaping Baryshnikov jacked on Dexedrine.

You have yours. Mine was Lauren.

• • •

She broke up with me in a pizza place in Kenmore Square in Boston, nearly ten years ago, just after a Red Sox game we'd gone to. I'd treated her to box seats to celebrate the two-year anniversary of our first date. We'd agreed to take a temporary "break" about six months earlier, but like with any first painful love, the hope for reconciliation was always there.

But over cold, flavorless pizza, she told me that she'd met somebody else. That she didn't love me anymore.

"It's not that I don't care about you," she intoned sweetly in that distinctive melodic voice of hers. "I just want to see what's out there."

Lauren.

She was one of those teeth melting sexy hotties with long auburn hair and librarian sunglasses. Like a Georges-Pierre Seurat–painted sunset, she was a million specks of goodness coming together to form a larger whole. A whole with boobies.

She had perfect succulent, soft abs that I would dust lightly with confectioners' sugar, then make a cup of tea. Her mammaries were wholesome and filling, swollen with divine purpose and baby-feeding agility. I would lead four-day hiking expeditions into those hills using only my cunning and trail mix to survive. I would nuzzle her upper arm area with my nose until the Northern Lights formed coherent sentences in Gaelic. I would powder my thighs with her discarded mascara and perform ass kabuki theater on the pavement outside her house as testament to those wondrous mounds of flesh. Anything for the chance to nibble her outer clavicle with a touch of soy sauce and wasabi.

She had nary a clue as to the power of her own hotness. But, then again, neither did I. I was too young to know what I had. Too naïve. "She's just the first," I thought to myself. I figured there would be more Laurens.

I took the train back to my new apartment in New York, where things got back to normal. I got a job. I dated. There were a number of subsequent hotties I had the pleasure to wrap in tinfoil and sauté in my love over a medium flame until they were bursting with lemon drop flavor. Sexy, urbane cuties whom I caressed with bamboo stalks and set goats on fire as a sacrifice to their curvaceous perfection.

But as the years passed, things kept going wrong. Something was off. Each of my new partners seemed as confused as Lauren was on the day she dumped me in Boston. They had the same restlessness, the same desire to dive back into the crowded swimming pool of mass culture and loud, music-pumping grindfests.

I sensed hottie wanderlust.

They were seized by the urge to test the bounds of their own worth on the hot scale. Endlessly trying to locate their value within a rapidly mutating culture defined by fashion magazine gloss. A never-ending race to grasp the brass ring, a veritable Donkey Kong of cultural barrel jumps. Always climbing. Always searching.

Where did they rank on the hottie scale? Which guy offered the best chance to prove their status?

And there he was, ready to sweep them off their confused little feet.

That new American male emerging from the swirling mix of club culture, product placement, suburban hip-hop and post-techno twenty-first-century image saturation. That cartoonish, skin-lotion-rubbing gym rat dancing shirtless to a techno beat and pumping his fists.

The douchebag.

Preening and aggressive. Oiled up and confident. Together with hot chick, these new dance floor couplings formed a cacophony of phony caca. Tribal tatts without a tribe. Designer dog tags. Bling, caps, tatts, and muscle tees—symbols of purchased identity. Performance over authenticity. Ritual instead of intimacy.

Tyler, my best friend from college, tried to explain it to me over beers in the East Village. Tyler had taken to getting his hair tips frosted for $200 at a salon and was hitting the gym four times a week. He was desperately trying to transform himself from a pudgy stock trader who worked on Wall Street into a pumped-up, tight T-shirt-wearing, ambiguously gay icon.

"Dude, it's like you're running a stock portfolio and the market's changed," he explained to me as we sipped Pabst Blue Ribbons at a bar on Avenue B. "It doesn't matter if a stock used to make you a lot of money. If those stocks start dropping, you gotta change your holdings, ya diggg?"

I eyed his shiny new dog tag necklace warily.

"It's a new world, bro," he said, clinking his glass against mine. "If you want the hottie, learn to douche it up or hit the bench."

"I'd rather hit the bench," I replied.

And I did.

I laughed off Tyler that day. But with every girl I dated, things began to get more confusing. They would giggle like schoolgirls when some oiled-up douchewank would knock into them and offer to let them try on his giant aviator sunglasses.

I knew I was in trouble.

I pondered the cultural change. Its shifting values. Its gender inversions and the spectacle of the masquerade. I thought about Tyler's ominous warning. And I thought about Lauren. I wondered what she'd been up to. What she was doing.

Until the day I ran into her.

Ten years to the month after our breakup. I was back home in Boston visiting my parents and, after failing to bum a ride from my Mom into Cambridge, I hopped on the 57 to Kenmore Square.

And then I saw her. At the front of the bus. Her shiny auburn hair was unmistakable, even from the back. But it was her laugh that sent shivers down my spine.

I pushed through the crowd of people to see if I could make out the guy she was with. It took a moment, but then Lauren leaned back and I got a glimpse of the hulking he-beast she was with. The primitive, grunting genetic misfire occupying space and air in her presence. His baseball cap was perfectly tilted, back and to the left. Back and to the left. Underneath the cap a giant blue bandana was tied tightly in a knot. His forehead was shiny and dripping, a mixture of hair gel and sweat. Two chain-link necklaces swung back and forth around his white muscle T-shirt. His surplus army shorts hung low and wide around his waist.

Lauren was dating a douchebag.

As this greased-up überchoad put his arm around my former girlfriend, the entire history of mankind's traumas paled in comparison with this singular wrongness. This giant, sucking vortex that screamed of a nihilistic and meaningless universe without compass. Without hope.

I watched as she got up and rang the bell for the next exit. Her smirking, stubbled choad made sure to readjust his baseball cap to its requisite ten-degree shift. Then he grabbed Lauren forcefully around the waist. His muscles flexed with dozens of tattoos. Chinese symbols. Barbed wire. A dragon. His extra-large shorts hung low, exposing a solid two inches of ass crack.

And there was Lauren. Enjoying it. Laughing.

She still hadn't seen me. I pressed myself into the corner of the bus, hoping to avoid detection. We rode onward for five minutes, five endless sixty-second cycles of a rhythmic tick-tock pounding in my head like bursting blood vessels.

Every manifestation of this oily scrotewank burned its douchey pattern into my retinas with the power of laser crystalline imprint. Every micron of his sweaty, greasy muscle T-shirt seared itself into my subconscious with the stamp of Freudian primal trauma. Of precognitive id-douche.

The bus pulled into a stop near Kenmore Square. As that douched-out abomination got off the bus, he slid his hands down Lauren's perfect back-side and lightly groped her perfect buttery butt of pure buttitude.

She giggled.

It hit me like a case of Grey Goose. Tyler was right. The stock market *had* shifted, and I was an investor without a clue. I sat transfixed in my seat, frozen with the horror of witnessing this cultural abomination. I felt dizzy.

But I had also glimpsed something transformative: my salvation.

I bussed it back to my parents' apartment and locked the door. I stepped over my childhood Colecovision that I'd hooked up to see if I could beat my old score at *Mr. Do's Castle* and fixed myself a bowl of Cocoa Puffs. The chocolate sugary goodness helped clear my mind and allowed me to focus.

I poured a glass of Night Train, my favorite cheap-ass wine, into a red plastic cup. It was going to be a long night. If I was going to deconstruct the codes of douchebaggery, I was going to need my strength.

I lay back on my bed.

I pictured her face again. Lauren. My Lauren. Lost to the dark forces of muscled douchebaggerchoad. No longer a person, but a concept. No longer an individual, but an emerging mission quest.

Like thousands before me, I had looked away too long. But no longer.

I pictured the millions of muscled-up club-going douchebags, posing for the camera with asstastic hand gestures, their arms hooked around some-one else's Lauren. Slowly, but with increasing certainty, it became clear.

I was to become the Catcher in the Douche-Rye. I was Beowulf, meant to slay the 'Bag-Grendel. I was the Savior of Hotties. The lone crusader on a journey into the darkest depths of the douchebag plague.

My quest would not be easy. To know douche, I would need to reach that most troubling of spiritual realizations that every man must confront in his quest for the curvy young hott-boobs: *The 'Bag Within*.

Like Siddharta, Jesus, and Batman before me, I would have to isolate myself in pure introspection. Only in my isolation could I hope for revelation. Only in meditation and contemplation could I find the power to confront the hottie/douchey plague once and for all.

THE MISSION QUEST

Exhausted, I spent a week without leaving my apartment. In order to spiritu-ally cleanse myself, I began a ritualistic purge in which I consumed only Oreos and organic goat's milk mixed with mint julep.

By the fourth night, I was too weak to pace the apartment. Slowly I crawled to the bathroom, where I collapsed on the floor. For hours I just lay there, staring up at the ceiling vents.

What could one person do against a societal plague of douchosity? My eyes drooped with fatigue. I could barely move my head. But Lauren was still out there, getting fondled by an assbag. Not just my Lauren. All of our Laurens.

Maybe it was the julep. Maybe that last Oreo's cream filling still stuck to the roof of my mouth. But it was then I heard it. A voice.

Ishmael!
"What?! Who's there?" I asked, jerking up to a sitting position.
Over here!
Startled, I glanced over at my bathroom countertop. It was then that I saw it.

My bottle of Vidal Sassoon hair gel. It had grown a large mouth right below its cap, and the mouth was talking to me.

I rubbed my eyes. Surely this was a hallucination.

It's not a hallucination, said the Bottle of Talking Vidal Sassoon Hair Gel.

"What do you want?" I asked.

Your mission is just beginning, Ishmael. You have examined The 'Bag Within. *Now you must confront* The 'Bag Without.

"Why do you keep calling me Ishmael?" I asked the bottle. "My name's Jay."

Ishmael, the douchebag waits for no one. He scrotes with impunity as we speak. He pollutes the hotties with his greasy charms at this very moment.

"But what can I do, Bottle of Talking Vidal Sassoon Hair Gel?" I pleaded. "I'm only one person!"

You have witnessed your Original Hot Chick with an überdouche. Now you must go out into the world with your realization and categorize every stage of the douche virus. You must record the history of douchebaggery and trace its permutations. Only then will you be free.

"But Bottle of Talking Vidal Sassoon Hair Gel, how? How can I do that?"

Start at the beginning, Ishmael. Start at the beginning of history and work your way forward.

I sat on my bathroom floor. I stared at the now quiet Bottle of Talking Vidal Sassoon Hair Gel, when it struck me: The Bottle of Talking Vidal Sassoon Hair Gel knew what it was talking about.

The Bottle of Talking Vidal Sassoon Hair Gel was right.

It was time to confront the hottie/douche plague once and for all.

I was ready.

Author's re-creation of event

Statue of Thessedouchuous, Greek philosophical wankscrote, 3200–3000 B.G. (Before Grieco)

CHAPTER 2

A HISTORY OF DOUCHEBAGGERY: FROM DOUCHE ANTIQUITY TO DOUCHE MODERNITY

Man is condemned to be douchey, because once thrown into the world, he is responsible for every douchey thing that he does.

—JEAN-PAUL SARTRE

TO UNDERSTAND MODERN douchebaggery, we must first look back at the historical record. The period known as *Douche Antiquity*.

Perhaps the most important piece of douchological evidence we have was uncovered in a cave in Galilee, Israel, during an expedition run by German archaeologist René Emile Belloq in 1981. The highly controversial third-century religious scroll, partially illegible and written on dried Papaya King leaves, suggests that douchey/hottie coupling was a troublesome facet of early societal religious structures. Here is a translated excerpt from the document that scholars are now labeling *The Gospel of Douchebagus*:

And douchebag begat douchebag, who begat douchebag, until the land was blessed with sweet nectar trees, plenty of oxen, and hot chicks with douchebags . . . [illegible] . . . And G-d watched with vague annoyance as douchebags spread across the land, bringing with them His word and a funky hip-hop beat with awkward white overbite dance moves. For within these pelvic thrusts and loud primal grunts as they tackled innocent Hotts who know not what they did, came forth the word of the Lord our G-d. And the Lord saw Douchebaggery. And it was "Woo!"

Another key piece of historical evidence of this period was the discovery of the linseed oil tapestries of Count Greasus the 'Bag in Italy in 1924. And when famed linguist Dr. Marcus Brody presented his translated lyrics from a fourth-century Gaelic folk hymn, "Shake that ass, Seamus!" at the Pan-Ireland Conference in Dublin in 1982, Douche Studies found renewed vigor among academic circles.

Primitive wall paintings discovered in the Staten Island dig of 1964

Some of the earliest inscriptions on record (50,000–60,000 B.G.) suggesting douchebaggery was frequent among primitive scrotal tribes

Scholars at the Johns Hopkins Department of Scrotology are perhaps the foremost experts in the field. Professor Marion Ravenwood was the first to theorize that primitive douchebags separated themselves from normative male development as early as the Armaniolithic period through the use of simple grunting and a sideways peace-sign hand gesture system. Ravenwood argues that this same grunting system still functions today in isolated tribes of Chad, Belize, and much of Orange County.

Ravenwood notes that one of the earliest recorded documents of douche subculture comes from the Kingdom of Kush in ancient Egypt. There we find numerous mentions among Theban King records of Seqenenra Tag, a ruler known as the "Guido of the Southern City." Seqenenra constructed large palaces where he would entertain his harems by, according to one translation, getting them to "back that junk up and get funky."

It is believed that the first douchebag hand gesture, the "Shock Like an Egyptian," was invented by Seqenenra during a period of intense consumption of fermented berry juice and hallucinogenic frogs.

Evidence during the Middle Ages is sporadic, yet there is enough to piece together a working hypothesis of medieval choadbaggery.

Theban King Seqenenra Tag, "Guido of the Southern City," pictured with Egyptian Hot Chick, 3250 B.G.

In 1098, Archbishop Anselm journeyed to Italy to plead with Pope Urban II to excommunicate what Anselm described as "tonguebags macking on the nuns." Anselm's scrolls state that eleventh-century teenagers from Tuscany, what he describes as "preening, pansy-ass, pretty boy, plucked-eyebrowed asswipes," had begun appearing in church services across much of southern Italy and were rivaling melanoma and syphilis as the leading causes of female sterility.

King Richard the Ballsack, painted in inverted 'bag sandwich formation, 1200 B.G.

Prince Munch of Choad, 1422 B.G.

Despite evidence of this rampant douchosity, Urban II refused a full ex-communication, preferring to simply make fun of the choad pimples at the weekly episcopal poker games.

England was also showing evidence of the douche effect. According to British archives, in the early Middle Ages in Dumfriesshire, Scotland, two young Scottish clansmen of the Scrotundae Clan were caught stealing crosses from a church built by Northumbrian aristocrats. As described in a local friar's journal, their goal was to wear the crosses as jewelry with which to "charm the stable wenches with my phat bling."

They were subsequently put on trial, degreased, and hanged.

Lord Kissy Lips of the Island of Long, 1432 B.G.

Galápagos ≈ 23 · North-Western inlet
A rare glimpse of the Sphinctiscus Mendouchulus,
the Galápagos Douche Penguins, during early
mating ritual.

8, 24 1831

Excerpt from Charles Darwin's sketches in
***On the Sub-Species of Douchitude.* Darwin's**
handwritten note reads: *A rare glimpse of the*
Sphinctiscus Mendouchulus, the Galapagos
Douche Penguins, during early mating ritual.
***8/24/1831* (159 B.G.)**

• • •

But England was not alone in noting douchebaguous development in the young males of their populace. In 1226, King Louis IX placed an official ban on all French youths attempting to "get their freak on" to minstrel melodies played in local horse stalls. Rumors of extensive mead consumption with the goal of "getting those fine French hotties to lez it up" caused Louis IX great consternation. This culminated with the infamous Lashing of Vinny incident at the Sorbonne in 1229, in which a young peasant was brutally punished for one too many shocker hand gestures in the presence of the Royal Court.

Nearly two hundred years after this incident, French historians note that the famous Ponce de León had discovered Florida while searching for the rumored Fountain of Douche. In 1535, Gonzalo Fernández de Oviedo wrote in his *Historia General y Douche de las Indias* that León was actually on a quest to find the rumored *Scent of Axe Bodyspray* as the means of curing sexual problems he was having with his wife, Jenny de León.

By 1575, Hernando de Escalante Fontaneda observed that León's douchebags could be found all over southern Florida. It is not certain, but the natives Fontaneda refers to could be the scrotal ancestors of today's oily Miami Beach überschlorts.

• • •

Anonymous photograph of frontiersmen pictured with unnamed douchebag (*left*), 1895 (95 B.G.)

By the late nineteenth century, during the frontier period in the American West, scattered reports of douchebaggery overtaking cowboys and infecting pioneer families were recorded. One journal, by a cobbler in Lubbock, Texas, describes an entire group of teenage men tilting their cowboy hats ten degrees to the left and donning polished horseshoes as necklaces. An anonymous diary from 1891 (99 B.G.) contained the following excerpt:

Tuesday, August 07, 1891
Chief Red Bull rode into town today and, after exchanging various tribal plants and resins for two polio-infested blankets, offered a warning to the outpost. While his English is still crude, Chief Red Bull made repeated references to someone he refers to as

The infamous Billy the 'Bag, 1886 (104 B.G.)

Dances with Douches. *We're not sure, but we believe he's referring to the corporal's son, Frankie.*

No record exists of Frankie's fate.

But perhaps the most famous example of late-period historical douchebaggery impacting world history was the assassination of Arch Douche Ferdinand I in 1914 (76 B.G.) by a furious Catherine the Hott, who'd caught Ferdinand making out in a castle bathroom with her former Best Friend Forever, Ashley.

This event started World War I.

FERDINAND
Archdouche d'Autriche.

Arch Douche Ferdinand I

• • •

After Arch Douche Ferdinand's assassination, 'bag/hott commingling, anecdotal and isolated throughout the historical record, began to surface in twentieth-century scrotal development. Today's modern douchebag (*Douchebagus scrotsus*), would not come into full maturation until the period that is now generally referred to as A.G., or *After Grieco*.

Historians argue over the exact year, but it is generally credited as between the fall of 1990 and the spring of 1991, when actor Richard Grieco achieved mass cultural influence through his appearances on the Fox television program *21 Jump Street*. This period, starting in the year 1990 (1 A.G.), is known as *Douche Modernity*.

DOUCHE MODERNITY

While 1990 (1 A.G.) is seen as the dividing line between Douche Antiquity and Douche Modernity, it is important to note that there were many cultural antecedents in the years prior to the arrival of the Grieco. For example, the fictional character Larry Dallas, Jack's swingin' upstairs neighbor on *Three's Company*. While Larry is not what we think of as a modern douchebag—he was relatively friendly and his accessories were relatively benign—we find some of the earliest significations of the modern douche persona within his construction. The hairy chest. The low-cut shirts. The desire to groom himself like some sort of inverted-masculine antithesis to Burt Reynolds machismo.

While the gender-bending glam-rock bands of the mid-1970s also featured some of the early douche markers that would eventually permeate mass culture, it was in the mid-1980s when modern douchitude began to become embraced by such bands as Ratt, Poison, and the extremely successful Guns n' Scrotses.

By the late 1980s, hair metal came under the influence of the emerging black hip-hop revolution. From hard-core urban gangsta to the mass-produced name brands in the suburbs, there was no greater influence during this awkward transition from late 1980s metal douche to early 1990s 'bag

Boston wankers New Kids on the Block, 1987 (3 B.G.)

maturation of the then-legendary Boston wankers New Kids on the Block.

All the classic signs of the modern douchebag were there among these five off-key toadbags; loud, colorful low-cut shirts and muscle tees, silly glittering necklaces and douched-out earrings, tilted baseball caps, spiked-up hair, and greased-up foreheads.

Complimenting the New Kids' white-boy, hip-hop douchosity was one-hit-wonder Latino singer Gerardo. Famous for his sleazy half-Mexican, half-American rap/dance 1991 douchefest "Rico Suave," Gerardo became one of the first fully-formed and complete douchebags of modernity.

Überdouche Gerardo, 1991 (1 A.G.)

Danny Bonadouchey

Gerardo's sleazy rap patter, his shirtless shaved chest, and his penchant for attracting leggy models sealed the deal. The 1980s glam rocker and urban rap ethos had become genetically cross-spliced into the greasy modern douchebag hybrid.

Like compatriots Menudo, Boys II Men, and iconic douche archetype Vanilla Ice, the New Kids and Gerardo were a powerful dual factor in ushering in the new age of Douche Modernity. The swirling noxious commingling of urban black subculture mixing with suburban white boy Tommy Hilfiger spoke to this new cultural paradigm. A societal shift of profound resonance. A societal shift that smelled like ass crack.

Richard Grieco, Prince of Douchitude

But these douchescrotes were not yet complete. There was one more stage of devolution to be undertaken: the Richard Grieco/Yasmine Bleeth coupling in the 1990s that would function as the archetype for all hottie/douche wrongness to follow.

This commingling of hottie Bleeth with Source Douche Grieco would produce a cultural effect, a societal ripple so profound that it would wrench us collectively into a state of full douche maturation by the mid-1990s and into the present day.

The Grieco is the conceptual dividing line between Douche Antiquity and Douche Modernity. The historical nexus point at which every trope of cultural meaning intersects, reinvents, and transforms from disparate unrelated events into a douche singularity.

For setting the standard of modern douchebaggery; for defining the oiled-up, sleazy überscrote; and for polluting the once pure and snowy Yasmine Bleeth, one cannot understate the importance of the hallowed greasechoad and occasional actor Richard Grieco.

But how did the Grieco come to occupy this hallowed and revered status within douchal hierarchy? For that answer, let us turn to the fairy tale that best explains the origins of Douche Modernity by telling the story of the original hottie/douche tragedy itself.

First discovered in a Zoroastrian book of folklore in 2004, the *Tragic Tale of Prince Grieco and Fair Maiden Bleeth* has been retold at campfire sites and in Euro-techno remixes. It has come to define the legend and myth that reverberates across all corners of the hottie/douchey spectrum.

Here, for the first time in print, is the official version of the legendary fairy tale that has come to define the modern hottie/douchey plague. The urban folktale that is the *Tragic Tale of Prince Grieco and Fair Maiden Bleeth*.

CHAPTER 3

THE TRAGIC TALE OF PRINCE GRIECO AND FAIR MAIDEN BLEETH

A LONG TIME ago, among the lush green hills and smoggy highways of a land called Tinsel, there lived a young and beautiful maiden. With auburn hair and plump, fantastic boobies of natural boobageness, this young beauty was known near and far across the lands as Fair Maiden Bleeth.

Fair Maiden Bleeth had found fame and fortune by filling out a red Baywatch swimsuit with hourglass curves, and an ass that wasn't no donkey. And whence she ran in slow motion on a beach with boobs that jiggled, the people across the land cheered with joyous arousal.

"Yay, Fair Maiden Bleeth!!" they shouted, as her bosoms shook and quaked with heroic inspiration and Jell-O Pudding Pop firmness.

"Run, Fair Maiden Bleeth!!" they cried, with leering glee.

And so she ran. With a life preserver and Hasselhoff by her side.

On days when Fair Maiden Bleeth would walk her Chihuahuas in Tinsel, noblemen, peasants, and model-actor, DJ, trust-fund asswipes would of-

fer to fall on their swords just to touch the hem of her miniskirt. Her natural beauty was dazzling.

And by natural, I mean all natural. No kidding. They's real. I mean come on. Look at those things. I'd sell my future infant daughter on the North African white slave market just to sniff their stethoscope after a chest exam.

But then one day, a mysterious tool rode into town. Famous across the land for his greased-up spiky hair, eyebrow makeup, and unholy obsession with wearing ultra-tight shirts and flexing his pecs, this was no mere farm-boy or Pilates instructor. For this was the knight known as Richard Grieco, Prince of Douchitude.

The Grieco with earlier conquest, Fair Maiden Applegate

Prince Grieco was the standard-bearer of a new type of prince that was sweeping across Tinsel: like a dark cloud or a pile of yak poo. A sudden and spontaneous appearance of douchebaggery the likes of which had never been seen before in all the many lands and forests.

The locals were troubled. Who was this mysterious douchebag? From whence had he come? No one knew.

But Prince Grieco cared not what others thought, for he was on a mission.

And so it was that Prince Grieco wooed Fair Maiden Bleeth with all the force his muscle tees and stubble could muster.

And, like many beauties before her, Fair Maiden Bleeth was no match for the power of a total and complete douchebag. Her youthful cries of "Woo!" quickly faded from her ruby-red lips and heaving swollen mounds of curvaceous perfection that I would juggle like greased-up hamsters.

And just like that, Richard Grieco, Prince of Douchitude, had claimed his princess.

And lo! Behold!

Clouds gathered and the heavens quaked with thunder. The sky grew dark *as frogs rained down. Collars across the land began to spontaneously pop.*

The gods had grown angry. For Fair Maiden Bleeth was far too sensuous and innocent—and had award-winning cans—to be in the presence of such rank and foul douche detritus.

But, alas. Alack. The people were powerless to stop the spreading dark darkness of dark douchebagguous dark.

Fair Maiden Bleeth had made her choice. She had chosen the 'bag.

Prince Grieco would hold Fair Maiden Bleeth in his 'bagalicious-movie-premiere-attending grasp for nearly four long, dark, and deeply scrotey years.

The people of Tinsel wailed and mourned. They gnashed their teeth. They rended their garments and cursed Ganesh. They wept for the loss of their beach-running maiden. But there was nothing they could do.

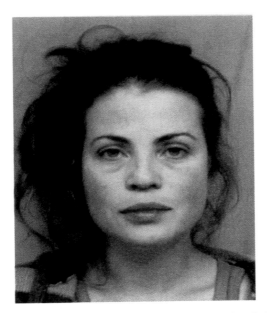

Fair Maiden Bleeth after her arrest by kingdom knights

After four years of enduring Prince Grieco's douchey ways, Fair Maiden Bleeth could take no more. She left Prince Grieco and took up with other douchebags. Two years later, out on her own and confused, Fair Maiden Bleeth suffered a tragic and horrifying downfall.

She was captured by the authorities of the king and prosecuted on charges of possession of the demonic spirit powder.

The people were shocked by her tragic downfall. And by tragic, they meant she was no longer that hot, because they were a shallow and petty people who read crap like InStyle magazine.

Little did Fair Maiden Bleeth know the price she would pay. The fate that awaits any young, perky-boobed maiden who chooses to follow the Path of the 'Bag.

The proximity of rank and foul douchebaggery had destroyed what was once so pure. Fair Maiden Bleeth was a fair maiden no more.

She was just Bleeth.

Bleeth faced her verdict as best she could. Her tearstained face betrayed her sadness. The king ruled justly, and Bleeth was sentenced to two years of probation and six weeks of mocking on Access Hollywood. Her once bouncy and firm tatines, which taste great with a side order of chili cheese fries, now drooped with sadness and neglect.

The once fair maiden had become despoiled. She had become what would henceforth be referred to across the land of Tinsel as Bleethed.

Young maidens of today, heed the warnings of Fair Maiden Bleeth. Grasp the moral of this tragic fairy tale. Glean the lessons of what can happen from exposure to deepest darkest douchebaggery.

You may think his glittery belt buckle is too sexy to resist. Or that his angry-young-man wife-beater shirt and scowling douche face are crying out for your attention.

But at what cost, fair maidens? At what cost?

Do not make the same mistake Bleeth made, fair maidens of the world. Listen to Bleeth's plaintive cry. Do not fall prey to the douchebag no matter how impressive his tribal tatts are.

Or you too shall suffer the dark, tragic fate of Fair Maiden Bleeth.

PART 2

THE STAGES, PERMUTATIONS, AND SCROTEY MANIFESTATIONS OF MODERN DOUCHEBAGGERY

We've covered the sordid historical origins of the hottie / douchey paradox. But before we continue to the present-day manifestations, I'd like you to repeat the following meditative de-douchification ritual with me:

1. Breathe in slowly through the nose.
2. Hold your breath.
3. Close your eyes.

4. Envision the last greased-up douche you saw in person.

5. Allow the rage to surface. Do not fight this emotional response.

6. Now picture the last boobilicious young plaything with bright doe eyes, succulent legs, and firm nectarine hindquarters who crossed your path.

7. Allow your rage to be slowly quenched in her angelic, soft-skinned glow.

8. Now slowly chant, "Armmmmmmmmannnnnnnniiiiiiiiiii . . . Exxxx-changggeeee . . ."

9. Exhale.

Good. Now we're ready to proceed.

CHAPTER 4

AM I A DOUCHE? NINE TELLTALE SIGNS YOU'RE TURNING DOUCHENESE, I REALLY THINK SO

THERE COMES a time in every scrotebag's life when he must choose—whether or not to bust out the unearned dog tags, the Ten-degree Hat Tilt, and the douche face. And, of course, the spiky cactus hair. He thinks, as every aspiring 'bag does, that such adouchrements will summon the hottie to his dark, sleazy flame, and then he makes the choice. He pulls that lever. He wanks that pud.

At that moment, he ceases to be all he once was. He becomes douchescrote. It is important for us to identify these most obvious and rudimentary markers of modern douchebaggery, the basic categories that help define the modern scrotepuddle.

There are nine main signifiers of douchechoadwank. Nine *tells*, if you will, that facilitate 'bag identification. They are the archetypal giveaways that quickly and clearly communicate the presence of douche virus within the young adult male.

However, we must be careful not to become too rigid in how we classify douche. Because, as with any subjective taxonomy, there is always an aesthetic component to the analysis. Many 'bags feature an unclassifiable quality, an *essence du 'bag,* that rises above specifics like ear bling, chin fungus, or teeth grillz. Therefore, identifying the douche is a process that is not only scientific, but also subjective.

The following pictures illustrate the elements of Source Douche in their most fundamental scrotey manifestations. Each stage, either by itself or in combination with other stages, identifies and defines douchebaggery. It is the starting point in the 'bag-identification, or tagging, process.

SIGN 1: THE POPPED COLLAR

One of the most important and basic giveaways of douchebaggery is the Popped Collar.

Nothing screams metrosexual 'bag quite like a pink or purple Polo or Izod short-sleeve shirt with an upturned collar amplifying the douche face.

Like a cloth spotlight, the Popped Collar announces: "Here there be 'Bag." It is a giant red-flashing warning light.

Popped Collar is found primarily on secondary and tertiary douche scrotewanks. It is rarely found on those dominating überdouche on the higher rungs of 'bag hierarchy who we'll see in the later chapters of this book.

We designate the Popped Collar as Sign #1 because it is one of the earliest steps a full-fledged douche takes as he embarks on his quest for hottie cuddle. As such, it is also one of the easiest markers to spot when 'bag hunting.

SIGN 2: JESUS BLING

Like the Popped Collar, another easily identifiable symbol of douche status is Jesus Bling.

Nothing shoots off scrotal flares of warning quite like a greased-up muscle tool wearing Playboy armbands attempting to claim some form of religious dedication while grinding his junk into a blonde hottie.

In the example pictured below, we see Jesus Bling in action. While he appears generally unthreatening, perhaps even nice, the necklace speaks to a dark side.

Like the Oracle at Delphi, Jesus Bling bespeaks a destiny of glittery, club-going douchebaggery. And while I'm no expert, I'm pretty sure Jesus didn't die to provide jewelry meant to accompany simulated public procreation.

But I may have misread the Gospel of Tony.

SIGN 3: UNEARNED DOG TAGS

One has to be careful when parsing out the dog-tag stage in case they're the actual dog tags worn by real veterans who have served in the Armed Forces.

Anyone who serves in the military, while not automatically guaranteed immunity from 'bag status (because 'bags are everywhere), certainly gets greater leeway. That said, designer douche tags aren't worn by vets, only wannabes. As such, like with the Jesus Bling, Unearned Dog Tags are a prime marker for identifying a choad playing tough-guy dress-up.

Take Top-Gun McDouche, pictured above. It is obvious to even the untrained 'bag hunter that the muscle tee, douche-fro, and double 'bag hand gestures are also in play. But it is the dog tag bling that first and foremost stamp this choadmunch as douche. Dog tags, like the Popped Collar and Jesus Bling, are quick giveaways of the presence of douche virus, and should be mocked accordingly.

As for Kato, his scrotal sidekick: Laugh it up, putz. Bra hottie just wants a free Cosmo.

SIGN 4: THE PHALLIC GREY GOOSE

The Phallic Grey Goose is a complex douche maneuver in which a 'bag simultaneously gropes a firm lower backside while proudly displaying his giant bottle of, well, Grey Goose vodka.

Much like the outbreak of crotch rash among the wildebeests of the Serengeti, the rapid spread of the Phallic Grey Goose maneuver began in Miami, Florida, in the early '00s, when a playah named Ricky first began utilizing the bottle as a euphemism for large male genitalia. From there it spread quickly, reaching epidemic proportions by late fall 2007. Scrotologists working deep underground in radiation-protected douche labs in Provo, Utah, remain perplexed at the rapid spread of the Phallic Grey Goose. No cure has yet been found.

The best response to the presence of Phallic Grey Goose is a simple but curt answer: *No, Ricky, I don't want to come back and* "partee like a rock steer" *in your suite at Sunset Tower.* But I will attempt to capture my own lambchop-ab cutie. For at least forty-three quality seconds.

Followed by a long awkward silence. And then turning on *Sportscenter*.

SIGN 5: TEN-DEGREE HAT TILT

While fading from its peak epidemic in late 2006, when it was estimated that between 10 and 20 million douchebags were tilting on a regular basis, Ten-degree Hat Tilt (10DHT) is still a signifier of the presence of douche.

And while it remains a cultural plague that rivals the Phallic Grey Goose, there are no Jerry Lewis telethons to raise money to treat 10DHT. No pleas from Sally Struthers to help "un-tilt the caps of the less fortunate." Yet it is a problem that continues to affect us all. Like lupus. Or pinkeye.

However, the medical term is a bit of a misnomer. Ten-degree Hat Tilt actually refers to a variety of presentational effects of a choadscrote's baseball cap. There is the actual Ten-degree Hat Tilt, of course. But variations also include 34-, 87-, and 112-degree tilt, as well as the extremely rare 27-degree tilt, pictured here.

Hat tilts that are nine degrees or less do not constitute an official marking of a 'bag, as the angular discrepancy can be ascribed to normal variance. But once a hat crosses the full ten degrees, the wearer must be 'bag tagged immediately. He has clearly chosen to announce douchebaggery. Thus he must be stamped as scrote.

The successful treatment of 10DHT will also play a key role in the de-douchification process, as explained in chapter 9.

SIGN 6: DOUCHE AURA

Sign #6, Douche Aura, differs from the first five signs in that it begins to move us away from object-based signs of douchitude to more conceptual ones. While the markers of name-brand products and douche gestures remain fundamental to 'bag hunting, there are other key factors at play: ethereal, abstract douchuousness.

Take Dimplebag, pictured here. His outward markings of 'baggery are limited to the stud belt and bizarre sabertooth-tiger necklace. While both are important signs of 'bag viral presence, there is another factor present that overrides the bling and communicates douchosity on a much more primal level: Douche Aura.

Simply squint your eyes and tilt your head. Now glance at the pic again. You'll gradually begin to see something flickering around the edges. Something that resembles a gelly, Axe Bodyspray-type, cloudy energy field.

Do you see it? That, is Douche Aura. Developing the keen ability to spot Douche Aura in the wild is one of the most important instincts a well-trained 'bag hunter will develop.

SIGN 7: THE DOUCHE FACE

As with Douche Aura, the Douche Face is one of the less easily identifiable, but still critical, giveaways of scrotological fungus in a 'bag.

Given that it is not an object-based marker, like the Popped Collar or Jesus Bling, Douche Face, like Douche Aura, can be harder to spot. But a keen 'bag hunter will know how to find its existence. Douche Face usually manifests itself in the presence of a digital camera, and only for brief periods. But once spotted, a trained 'bag hunter will know that he or she has tagged a 'bag successfully.

For an aspiring 'bag hunter still untrained in 'bag tagging a douche face, one giveaway is that it often appears in the presence of large, succulent flesh pillows. Amateur 'bagologists should camp near a gaggle of pillows and wait. Usually within minutes a douche face will appear.

Douche Face variations include pouting, tongue display, crinkling the brow, and of course—the infamous douche sneer, first developed by the oily Island Pioneers of Great Neck, Long Island, in the late 1980s.

SIGN 8: THE SHINY FOREHEAD

The ratio between 'bag and forehead shine is not a linear one. It is more like an exponential douchesplosion. For every degree up the grease scale we go, douchitude increases by a factor of ten.

As excessive hair product naturally produces a sheen-like glow on the forehead, this is a dead giveaway for the presence of douche virus. As such, Sign #8 is one of the more easily spotted of the nine basic signs, but still requires attention to detail to observe.

In the forehead shine is also what scrotologists refer to as the Mark of the 'Bag. This is when the forehead glint appears to form a complete set of male genitalia, as seen on the Brad Pitt Choad pictured here. And when I say complete set, I mean all the elements that make up the team. The king and the pawns. The Santa and the elves.

A trained 'bag hunter will be able to tell the difference between simple forehead sweat and a fully reflective douchal shine. Even if the Mark of the 'Bag has not taken on the shape of male genitalia, an experienced 'bag spotter will be able to parse the ratio of gel crust, grease, bodyspray, and fake tan residue that form the refractive spectrum of true forehead grease. As such, a 'bag hunter may need to wait for proper shine reflection, in the right club lighting, before making this douchal determination. And by determination, I mean a collective "ew."

SIGN 9: THE MISSING SHIRT

There's an automatic guideline when determining 'bag status in relation to shirt removal.

Unless one is on a beach, putting out a brush fire, or getting a mole exam, the removal of one's shirt in the presence of an attractive young woman is an A-1 ticket to ride on the Douchey-Go-Round. You are auto-scrote. You are douchewank.

Take the Jesus Bling-wearing Miami Vice pictured here. Sure, he's muscular. But I haven't seen breasts that pale since I had the garlic chicken at the Olive Garden. I don't care how many free breadsticks and salad you get, honey. Send it back.

So consider this a fixed rule of 'bag taxonomical categorization: Inside the club, no shirt equals automatic 'bag. Do not pass "Go." Do not collect two hundred tribal tatts. You have caught a douche.

CHAPTER 5

AM I DATING A DOUCHE? THE CATEGORIES OF MODERN DOUCHEBAGGERY

Today we tested the first blast. The power was beyond our imaginations. Although I witnessed the event from over a mile away, I could swear I saw the contours of a face in the fiery explosion. The pink base resembled a person's upturned collar. And the tip of the mushroom cloud took on the round shape of a young man's head. A giant cactus head. Oily, with spikey hair and a smug expression. I felt God himself was warning me. The power of this new weapon was as destructive as that of a pure douchebag.

—ROBERT OPPENHEIMER, MAY 1942

NOW THAT WE'VE established the nine basic signs of douchebaggery, we can begin to classify the various stages that is the modern hottie/scrotey plague. But before we enter this fetid swampland, we must understand that douchuousness is not simply what one wears or looks like.

It also comes from *within*.

In this way, douchosity is more than simply the items found on or gestures made by the individual scrotewank we saw in Chapter 4. It is in the captured performance, that moment when a camera flashes, when a third party witnesses the Scrote/Hott in stylized douche action, that 'bag meaning is both created and amplified.

This brings up a number of compelling metaphysical, spiritual, and hair gel-encrusted questions. Between object and subject, where is 'bagject? At which point in space/time do Fratbags, Tonguebags, Guidobags, and Yuppiebags converge into a singularity of douche, a black hole of such gravitational force that neither grease nor bling can escape?

We must locate douchitude not as a singularity, not as a point in space/

time, but as a binary relational trope. As a counterpoint. As intertextual symbiosis.

Thus, to properly reflect on douche effect—to find this truth—we must use both 'bag and his counterpart: the hottie. Only when we comprehend both douche and hottie together, commingling in so many nauseating and spiritually disturbing ways, will we find true illumination of the illogical nature of all things boobie/scrotey. For without such a powerful dialectic, we are but lost travelers in an endless metaphysical Armani/Exchange clearance sale, without a credit card.

The douche leads us toward darkness. But the boobuous light of hottie leads us out. Only when they are *together,* mixing, swirling like a toxic cock-tail of both hope and disease, of purity and poo, will we find revelation.

So let us continue our examination of contemporary douchebaggery within this coupling of douchitude and hottitude. Together. Improbably in-tertwined. Illogically enmeshed. For it is between their polarities that we will find truth.

THE FRATBAG

Like amoebas, cockroaches, or Starbucks coffee shops, Fratbags are everywhere. Ubiquitous. Scrotorious. They are the base douche. The Soylent Green of the 'bag diet.

Fratbags are usually found traveling in large twelve-packs of broad douche samplings, and will often run the gamut of douchological classification in a single scrum. Pictured here we have everything from Ten-degree Hat Tilt to the Celticbag. Rampant are bling, facial configurations, douche hand gestures, as they line themselves up in a row that cries out for societal mocking: this is a typical Fratbag gaggle.

Fratbags are considered harmless and can usually be dissuaded from excessive female bothering by the presence of loud hip-hop, a professional sporting event, or alien slugs that lay eggs in their brains.

The hottie, pictured here, functions as a counterpart. She is pure like snowflakes no one could ever stain. She smiles sweetly, as the Fratbags make hand gestures. Within this oscillation between hottie and choad, douche meaning is found.

A desire to explore pink stalactite mountains on a fever dream of self-discovery. A dream where you nuzzle the warm fleshy hills, chant the rhythmic Om, search your chakra, and discover a higher consciousness. A higher boobie consciousness.

THE FEDERBAG

Another of the fully formed college scrotes, slightly more toxic than the Frat-bag, is the Federbag. The Federbag impersonates the D-List actor/rapper/ex-husband of whichever pop-culture douchelebrity is in vogue. By emulating the trends of talentless gossip-rag fodder, the Federbag hopes to appeal to hotties by displaying his celebri-echo. His reappropriation of a culturally validated celebrity image.

Federbags, although not actually famous, use such powerful image reconstruction as to render the Federbag an actual douche celebrity. These D-list wannabes spend their unemployed years emulating their tabloid head-lining progenitors while burning through trust funds and credit cards.

Famous in their own minds, they live the celebrity rock-star lifestyle while being neither celebrity nor rock star. Just pud.

THE HOVERBAG

Whenever a combination of faux-lesbian hotness spontaneously forms, there's a bizarre natural apparition that appears behind them. This artifact consists of hovering douchitude that seems to manifest instantly out of thin air: the Hoverbag.

These Ghostscrotes appear in a translucent douche state, hover briefly with a blank, vaguely lobotomized expression, often make monosyllabic comments like "Lesbos!" and "Sweet!," and then vanish without a trace.

Science is baffled by this effect. Unofficially referred to by scholars of the Douche Sciences as *Hoveringus douchus*, this variant of the Northern

Douchey Lights has defied rational explanation and inspired guttural cries of, "Get out of the picture, Hoverdouche!" for decades.

However fleeting their manifestation, Hoverdouches still require stiff kicks to the groin for ruining the show.

THE TONGUEBAG

The Tonguebag functions as an instant scrotal 'baglump—all within one simple, yet sleazy, gesture. Tonguebags can be identified in action only, not through dress, bling, or hair. As such, tonguebaggery works as a gateway drug for an aspiring 'bag taking his first steps into a larger world of creepy awkwardness.

Yet tonguebags often are dabbling in the douche arts, only to retreat to generic normalcy moments later. As such, they stand on the dividing line between 'bagling and fully-formed choad. But the moment a camera captures such early douchitude, the Tonguebag betrays his scrotal tendencies. He makes the tiniest gesture that's a crucial window into his 'baggy soul.

If a Tonguebag is not careful, excessive chest gel, Ten-degree Hat Tilts, and bizarre facial pubes await in his dark, douchey future. Tonguebaggery can often be that first greasy step into a larger world of scrotal douchuousness. As such, the Tonguebag is not to be taken lightly by the experienced 'bag hunter. He should be mocked by calling him *poo*.

THE KISSY LIPS

One key giveaway of a fully-formed douche are the Kissy Lips. This aesthetic violation of all that is humane in a sane and just universe should be apparent to even the least professionally trained 'bag hunter.

The urge to smack Kissy Lips with a soggy rye dipped in the Hudson River is primal, basic, and undeniable. However, like the Tonguebag or the Douche Face, Kissy Lips has its own specific subsection of douchebag categorization.

Kissy Lips douche face is spiritual malfeasance. It is cruel and unusual punishment for even the most hardened douche hunter.

But as with any yin-yang polarity, the cutie offers us hope. The cutie calls to us to curl up and drift off to sleep in her soft, freshly powdered glow, while stuffing enchiladas up our noses. Because nothing's hotter than stuffed-enchilada nose.

ROCKY 'BAGBOA

Rocky 'Bagboas are an important and distinct subsection of douche hierarchy. They're not classifiable simply as muscle choads, nor pumped-up 'roidbags. They are something else entirely.

The key to this distinction lies in the 'Bagboa's ability to simultaneously possess and present their hottie with the pride of heroic accomplishment—as if he had engaged in some form of metaphorical douche ram-butting-heads contest and triumphed heroically. And all to the swelling trumpets of a cheesy 1970s orchestral accompaniment.

Take the 'Bagboa featured here. Rocky's got the smirk down, stone-cold bad-ass style. And by stone-cold bad-ass, I mean poseur choad douchebag.

A proper 'bag hunter should match his gaze with icy Mr. T coldness, then mock his shirt with blazing sarcasm while two ten-year-olds hold up a misspelled sign in the background.

However, Ring Girl is twelve rounds of card-holding goodness. You should desire to discuss Frazier/Ali in a smoky gym on Tenth Avenue while wearing a 1970s tweed jacket if it meant you could nibble on her boxing gloves in the back sink area when she wasn't looking.

Which is another way of saying you find her attractive.

SIR PECS-A-LOT

Sir Pecs-a-Lots are an increasingly common form of 'Bagboa-like douche-baggery: the pumped-up muscle scrote.

However, the Sir Pecs-a-Lots are distinguishable from Rocky 'Bagboas by the way they present the hotties. Sir Pecs-a-Lots focus far more on their own physicality than on the female prize.

One key distinctive feature of Sir Pecs-a-Lot is that he knows how to mark his territory using clear and unambiguous physicality. Observable in the wild, Sir Pecs-a-Lot uses primal grunts so that neighboring tribes will know not to approach his female, share his drinking water, or urinate on his trees.

Later, Sir Pecs-a-Lot plans to stare confusedly at a mysterious black club entrance door, while triumphant classical music plays. Suddenly it will come to him, in a flash of recognition. A bone can also function as a tool.

A douche tool.

THE EUROBAG

Eurobags present a distinct otherness within their performative douchosity. Their wanky scrote is still clearly douche, but something about it is foreign. Exotic. And by exotic, I mean puketastic.

Eurobags' plastic skin oozes of Nordic butter crèmes and Tuscan hair gels, and their shirts smell vaguely of Toblerone and Riccola. They grin at us as if to say, "Hey, I may be from Antwerp, have no chest hair, and get mistaken for a female bull dyke on occasion, but that's just me."

A fully lathered-up work of Renaissance art, the Eurobag inspires international post-Colonial douche rage across much of the subcontinent. His nasal accent sings with indeterminate hotel-lobby resonance.

With foreheads gleaming in the setting sun like the ancient Norwegian fjords, and hair spiked like southern Spanish spring dew glitter, the Eurobag dances like only he can dance.

THE GREASY EURO-DOUCHE

Not to be confused with the Eurobag, the Greasy Euro-Douche isn't even European at all. He just smells like Europe. By which I mean unshowered and oily.

Greasy Euro-Douche helps demarcate the cross-cultural global spread of metro-douche trend lines. Much as earthquake seismologists study fault lines for global impact, we must observe not only the specificities of douche manifest but also their inter-relational cross-cultural reflective pull.

Simply put, the Greasy Euro-Douche confirms an important fact of viral douchitude: It's gone global. In the example here, note the key second unbuttoning of the solid-color rayon dress shirt. Scrotologists note that this douche trend was actually started in a small ski chalet in Rekjavik by a nineteen-year-old ski instructor named Klaus. Charting these movements—from America, to Europe, and back to America again—become key to determining which rectal projects are categorized as Euro-Douche and which fall into other distinct classifications.

In other words, time to bomb Dresden again.

THE BEATERBAG

One of the classic visual signifiers of the bar-crawling assmunch, perhaps the clearest way to announce "I am scrote!" outside of removing the shirt, is the "wifebeater + bling" look.

Wifebeaters have their place: boxing movies, porn, gay gyms in West Hollywood.

But in public? Unless your armpits are being treated for crotch rash, there is no excuse for donning a wifebeater. Especially in the presence of the hot.

But the Beaterbag has another goal. He aims to communicate the visual codes of hip-hop urban style. Although, to the rest of us, it communicates steaming yak vomit.

Hottie here is the perky younger sister of your college girlfriend who you thought about in surreal fantasies you didn't even admit to your therapist. But you can admit them to me. Because I care.

THE NAVAJO MUD TOY 'BAG

The Navajo tribe of New Mexico used to make mud toy figures for their children to play with. These intricately constructed figurines were some of the most douchey folk art ever produced by the indigenous people of the Americas.

Here we see a Navajo Mud Toy 'Bag come to life, perhaps animated by the legendary Najavo spirit, River Douche. Note the swollen clay head and fixed, creepy stare. Navajo Mud Toy 'Bag has found his way into a nightclub, where he's attempting to tackle two lovely marshmallow bunnies who are sending up smoke signals of surrender.

When spotting a Navajo Mud Toy 'Bag, do not confront his claymated existence. Instead, simply call a shaman to purge the douche spirit from this large pile of animated clay before it is too late.

After neutralizing a Navajo Mud Toy 'Bag, it is appropriate to rain dance for hours just for the chance to rub tantric tribal oils on the hotties' upper elbow areas until one of them hits you on the head with a candlestick.

THE GANGSTABAG

One of the dangers of observing the Gangstabag, aka Hip-hop Scrote, in his natural habitat is the off chance that you're actually mocking a real-life, gun-toting homie. As the designer brands and legit hoodlum looks converge, distinguishing the various permutations of douchebag impresarios from the real bust-a-cap-in-my-ass homies becomes an arduous task indeed.

Is this one of the many wannabe Miami Beachites attempting to pull hottie tail with imagined stories of *Scarface*-inspired drug deals on the south side? Or is this dude an actual drug mule for the Corleone family's Cuban connection?

If the latter, let me state that Gangstabag is a scholar and gentleman, and I would sip Vietnamese sugar teas with him while reading Beckett.

I would then drink fresh squeezed orange juice off chicka's shoulder blades until my scurvy was cured.

THE ROCKERBAG

There is a certain leeway of douchal expression allowed in successful rock musicians. If you have a #1 album and want to douche it up Kid Rock–style, you're a still a 'bag—but a 'bag who actually earned the right to be 'bag.

But then there are the Rockerbags. Like the Federbag, they are imitations—everyday choads with day jobs and weekly gigs at O'Mally's, playing U2 covers for free beer.

Take Hang Loose Rockerbag, pictured here. Leather wristband. Überdouche face. Utilizing the horns hand gesture, the Rockerbag says, "Look at me; I rock!" This male version of the female "Woo!" mating call signals the desire to perform coitus.

For the most part, Rockerbags represent a benign and relatively harmless subsection of scrotastic asstitude. They're not "not douche enough" to not call them douche, but they're not douche enough to call them überdouche either. And by not "not" I mean not. And by boobies, I mean breasts.

THE ALL-AMERICAN 'BAG

A basic staple of standard 'bag, categorization is the classic All-American douchescrote. The apple pie 'bag. The preppy tool. The collegiate wank.

All-American 'Bags are mostly found congregating in the central and southern United States, state schools like Michigan and Ohio State, and a whorehouse in southern Paraguay called the *Can-Can*.

The All-American 'Bag is one of the subtler 'bag manifestations. There are no obvious giveaways or over-the-top markers.

And yet, the Douche Aura of the All-American 'Bag confirms a deeply emanating scrotal rot. Like Fratbags, All-American 'Bags don't really threaten, but are still annoying enough to categorize.

And by categorize, I mean make fun of for making gang signs while wearing tinsel and argyle.

THE JERSEYBAG

A Jerseybag is not always literally a douche from New Jersey, although there can be obvious connections. Like, well, being from New Jersey.

But a Jerseybag is actually a state of mind: a cultural cocktail of swill reared in the big-hair, Bon Jovi–arena rock concerts of the late 1980s and post–Dice Clay cries of male scrotal grabbing. It's a persona forged in the dark fetid swamplands of Italian sandwich shops and suburban strip mall malaise. Devils fans and Springsteen. Exit 16W.

Jerseybags are generally harmless. They're loud and obnoxious, but generally harmless. That being said, beware of the neck muscles. They bulge. Oh, yes. They bulge greatly. Like Henry Rollins or African goiter.

Pocahontas Hottie, pictured above, remains blissfully unaware of her proximity to Jersey choadbaggery. Her innocent smile and sweet demeanor could cure shingles. Like a crisp French onion soup, a true 'bag hunter would partake with the hunger of a prisoner reared on government cheese. They would indulge like Gandhi after a six-day meditative fast. They would cover their foreheads with bacon strips and head butt into her like an angry ram until she screamed, "Yahtzee!" in a nasal Welsh accent.

AQUABAG

Aquabags can be extremely difficult to spot in the wild. They must be observed plying their douche trade in either a swimming pool or Jacuzzi for proper scrotological categorization.

In their natural habitat, Aquabags will swim up on unsuspecting females and bust a variety of primal mating calls, including: "Pretty sweet pool, huh?", "What room are you hotties staying in?", or "Yo, want a Miller Lite?" These calls are quickly followed by extensive grunting and crotch-scratching.

Here we see one of the rare Aquabags, the *Aquadouchus shavedus*, in action. This is a mutant hybrid from the head-shaving scrotological movement of early 2006.

Note the Aquabag's complex use of 'bag hand gesture signals. These communicate to fellow Aquabags to stay away from the Woo-Hotties he has now staked his claim to. Aquabags are often observed posing in simultaneous attack/mating positions. Their presence in water is usually due to hunting hotties, consuming mass quantities of Miller Lite, and/or urinating obsequiously.

FURRY HEAD 'BAG

Furry Head 'Bags often appear benign and unthreatening—more laughable than disruptive. But do not let their silly furry heads conceal their true douchological presence.

Because Furry Head 'Bags mock our collective achievements. Furry Head 'Bags laugh at our puerile attempts to rise above primordial base instincts and ascend to higher plateaus of consciousness.

Furry Head is the grounding force of reality. The check on human gravitas and self-ascribed importance. The slap in the face, the dash of cold water, the sobering and uncanny reminder that the only emotion we should ever partake in when contemplating our role in the universe is this one: humility. And laughter at Furry Head.

So perhaps we should thank Furry Head. For Furry Head retells the story we need to constantly be retold. The delusional folly of self-importance. The reminder to be humble in the face of a vastness that blinks once and we're here. Blinks twice, and we're gone.

Or he's just a douche with really silly hair.

THE PUNKBAG

This white, suburban co-opt of the '80s punk/hard-core look may be one of the more annoying offshoots of the douchebaggery tree.

Punkbags personify the store-bought attempt to use name brands to acquire the artifice of punk authenticity. These are actions that would've caused true punks to toss them through windshields, and then go for pizza.

Archie McDoucheface, fun with a bottle of peroxide and a chain-link bracelet does not make you Sid Vicious. Douche hand gestures in the presence of Love Hottness only render you a 'bag.

So take your illegally burned Buzzcocks CD, your overpriced retro Vans, your well-worn copy of Legs McNeil's *Please Kill Me* and, well, please kill yourself.

Superfly Love Hott looks like that girl on the college volleyball team who you'd watch work out in sweats out of the corner of your eye while pretending to study the campus bulletin board. The kind you'd take an economics course with in the vain hope that she'd ask you to study with her. But she never did. Because you're a moron.

THE BUDDHABAG

Buddhabags are a relatively unthreatening form of douchecrud. The key identifier of the Buddhabag is the exhibition of a preternatural Zen calm in the presence of the hott. There is a stoic, almost meditative state of repose that seems to say, "I am above such petty worldly desires like the boobie."

But they are not above the boobie. Look closely and an experienced 'bag hunter will find the giveaways. In this case, the douche face.

Note to all aspiring Buddhabags: When the hotties are *paid* to pose with you, do not make the douche face. You are not a bad-ass. You did not score four cuts of hott any more than the waitress at Hooters actually thinks you're sexier than the rest of her customers that day.

And yes, we all have the friend who thinks the stripper/Hooters waitress/paid promotional hottie actually "likes me, dude!" Hint: She doesn't. No, not even because of the anecdote you're citing. She still doesn't.

THE ORANGEBAG

Like the Popped Collar, the Orangebag is a primary color within the douche rainbow. It is a standard scrotal category into which we dip our brushes to paint the higher and more nuanced categories of douche hierarchy.

In evaluating an Orangebag, a number of important theological, epistemological, and scatological questions arise. Does a man-tan ripen when water is added?

If we planted an Orangebag's head in some soil, would we grow oranges?

Or would they be yams?

Or would a giant douche tree grow that would sprout gel-flowers every spring with that lovely odor of Axe Bodyshots mixed with a hint of orange Gatorade? Perhaps we should just ditch the spud and order a pizza.

THE REDNECKBAG

Redneckbags occupy an uncertain status within douche hierarchy because—who are we kidding?—rednecks couldn't score a hottie with a branding iron and sixteen piglets for trade.

However outside the realm of scrotal achievement they may be, Redneckbags must be accounted for. And by accounted for, I mean have their ridiculous 'staches and dirty sleeveless T-shirts mocked in book form.

Acceptable responses to witnessing a Redneckbag in public include moonshine waterboarding, spontaneous defecation, or simply pelting the dude in the face with a package of Funyons.

Redneck's counterpart, the Red Hott, often appears to be a dark and sultry wine of mature, over plumped berry. The kind you would jump into a bathtub full of electric eels wrapped in tinfoil just to rub her acting audition tapes on your inner thigh in highly inappropriate ways. Of course, why electric eels would be wrapped in tinfoil is something you still haven't figured out.

THE SAGGY PEAR

When I was a little kid, my dad and I lived near Haymarket, a farmer's market in downtown Boston. Every Sunday the fruit and vegetable guys would be out selling whatever crates they had left over from the week.

They lined up their trucks and would sell to anyone who'd be willing to go through all the saggy and overripe product to find the good ones mixed in there. Or give 'em two bucks and take the whole thing.

My dad and I would buy an entire box of cucumbers and then dig through and pull out eight or nine fresh ones like we'd won the lottery. We'd tally up how much each would've cost in the supermarket and figure out how much we'd saved with our Sunday morning ingenuity. It was part bargain hunt, part weekend activity.

Once we bought a box of pears that appeared OK when we glanced at it, but when we went through it, it was completely unsalvageable. It was the only time that had ever happened. We'd only paid a few bucks for it, but still. We were always able to find at least five or six perfectly good fruits or vegetables in the box. In this case, not one. This time they were all rotten, saggy, and moldy.

Which brings me back to the saggy pear douche. Droopy, moldy, generally unsalvageable douchitude in the presence of a tasty drink of water.

But hey, at least this rotting pear brought back a fond memory.

So there's that.

FALL OUT 'BAG

Like the indie rock group that shares this pud's moniker, Fall Out 'Bags remind us of that college European history major who talked too much in class and smelled like sock sweat.

You know the type. The C student whose parents financed an extensive wardrobe of vintage clothing. The senior who partied like a rock star, snagged the innocent and sweet pre-med hotties who everyone fantasized over, and spent the next twelve years stocking crates at Best Buy while trying to get his band, The Arthritic Tics, off the ground.

As such, Fall Out 'Bags inspire annoyance far beyond the actuality of their douche manifest. Their six-inch gelled hair and eyeliner are merely signs of a future of dollar tips and bar-counter wipedowns. But, like the Rockerbag and the Federbag, they live the rock-star lifestyle in search of a hottie to fool with dazzle. And so they are douche.

TICKLE ME EMO

Tangentially related to the Fall Out 'Bag, the Tickle Me Emo is a variation, the art-douche subsection of 'bag classification.

We all know the Tickle Me Emo—those weird dudes smoking in the quad during lunch, or gender ambiguous, "too cool to care" asswanks who occasionally seem able to pull former cheerleaders during their rebellion phase without any apparent effort.

The Tickle Me Emo example, pictured here, summons the ghost of Morrissey by way of Elvis Costello. He plays The Decembrists on shuffle on his iPod while summoning the ethos of Jason Schwartzman in *Rushmore*.

The key to tagging a Tickle Me Emo is the anti-'bag aesthetic. The lack of caring, only to douche out in so many subtle ways. But anti-'bags are still 'bags, let there be no doubt. They simply invert the scrote and douche from within.

Or course the lack of effort is their effort. They're like anti-'bag douche. And, like anti-matter, they punch holes in the fabric of space/time. Or at least smack us in the face with a large dead porcupine.

THE ARTBAG

Artbags are the urban hipster next-level douchery. They're Emobag or Fall Out 'Bag all grown up into a state of full scrotal maturity.

Signs of overt 'baggery in the Artbag are not always as obvious as Jersey-level regurgitation. Instead, Artbags are subtler, more sensitive.

Originating in San Francisco during the late 1990s Internet bubble (see *Rise and Fall of the Scrotuman Empire*), Artbags developed like a fungal bark mushroom growing on the tree trunk of human achievement. These douchechoads can be spotted taking up habitat in loft spaces and warehouses in crime-ridden districts, and naming their purebred French bulldog "Napoleon" or "Derrida."

Artbags practice their douchey charms away from prying cameras and do not announce their presence easily. Like Curie, Pasteur, or Bruce Banner, a 'bag hunter must first isolate the contagion before exposing it to the purifying light of the collective mock.

Artbag hotts are capable of inspiring some 'bag hunters to light bonfires in the dried cackle brush of the Serengeti until the smoke clouds summon the rare white-tailed mongoose. The 'bag hunter would then explain in graphic and lurid detail to that mongoose how much they'd like to lick the dark lace bobby socks of Jenny McBlonde's Southern Texas perfect upper bicuspids.

But the mongoose wouldn't understand what they're saying. Since mongooses don't speak English.

THE HIPSTERBAG

The Hipsterbag, an offshoot of the Tickle Me Emo and the Artbag, is an increasingly disturbing phenomena in recent douche hierarchical development.

The Hipsterbag works along a complex pathology, utilizing more ideologically-based tropes than your traditional popped collar and spiky-haired tool. Giveaways include douchey facial hair, annoying ironic T-shirts like "Free Winona" or "Free Paris," and, of course, the emotionally detached douche-face that says, "I'm here but I'm not really here. Because I'm too ironic to commit to actual emotions."

Enough, Hipsterbag.

We don't want to hear about the band you're starting without a bass player but featuring your musically untrained Parsons classmate playing a 1982 Casio keyboard into a microphone.

We don't want to read your 'zine.

We're not going to invest in your Web-design company.

We don't want to hear about the time when you hooked up with Teal and smoked from a hookah at an outdoor cafe before retiring to her loft apartment to have unsatisfying sex to her Belle and Sebastian records. On vinyl.

SCROTIO RISING

Scrotio Rising is an example of the mystical branch of douchological study, Douchestrology. Capturing all twelve stages of Douchestrology is an extremely difficult effort, and should not be attempted by the amateur 'bag hunter.

Only one extensively trained in Douchestrological readings is able to parse and catalogue all twelve scrotal signs.

In reading the douchestrological signs pictured here, forty-degree hat tilt is generally located within Scrotio Rising. Eighty-degree hat tilt would place this picture on the douchological charts closer to the *Dawning of the Age of Scrotarius*.

However, the revelation of underwear over two inches in girth means that the moon is between choad and fratbag. And by moon, I mean douche ass.

An experienced Douchestrologist can project his or her deepest reading techniques on any image of festering douchitude. In this way, the trained douchestrologist can predict the future, the past, and the ass-pimple.

Thus, you can see the complexities of the Douchological read. Do not attempt to do a reading without purchasing the famed mystical text on Scrotology, *Chariot of the Scroads*.

And, of course, the two firm solar globes hovering delightfully on this Zodiac pixie stick are confirmation of the star patterns of boobology that fit in perfectly with Scrotio Rising's charts. They confirm that you would spend a solid minute of awkwardness attempting to dawn her Aquarius and Pisces her Gemini until she called over her older brother to come and kick your ass.

Which he wouldn't.

Because you'd hide under the sofa and refuse to come out.

INDIANA SCROTE AND THE TEMPLE OF HOTT

Throw me the hottie; I throw you the cheeseburger!

It's probably obvious that Indiana Scrote is relatively harmless. He's possibly even a nice guy. But this monarch of the sea does exemplify a certain category of base-level wankpuddery. He's a douche adventurer on a quest for delicious lambchop legs, all while affecting the persona of conquering explorer.

The Temple of Hott, pictured here, is a Brooke Burke Covenant. Her arcs are a transmitter, a radio for speaking to God. When witnessing a hott this hot in the presence of an Indiana Scrote, it is normal to desire to challenge her to a whiskey shot contest while shoving the Staff of Ra six ka-dam's up Indiana Scrote's whip.

Not because he's that douchey. But because she's that hot.

THE DOUCHE FLY

I have traveled to many places in my short time on this Earth.

I've hunted Caribou in Nunavut and the Northwest Territories. I've played blackjack for rum while stowing away on illegal spice-trading missions off the coast of Uruguay. I've fought alongside Henry Darger and the Vivian girls in the Realms of the Unreal during the Glandeco-Angelinnian war storms caused by the Child Slave Rebellion.

But the one constant throughout so many of my adventures in 'bag-fighting and hottie-saving has been the Douche Fly. He's buzzing, annoying and distracting, ever present throughout the world. The Douche Fly moves too quickly to swat. He's always out of reach, yet refuses to leave.

Douche Flies don't always demonstrate noxious and potent distilled douchebaggery. But they're always buzzing. They're a somewhat ethereal section of modern douchebaggery, but their scrotitude remains an annoyance nonetheless. Douche Flies are not particularly douchey. They're more like the catch-all categorization for unidentifiable douchebaggery. But they buzz. And so, we mock.

THE ABACRAB

Unlike the Douche Fly, Abacrabs are one of the most potent douchebags. Abacrabs need to exhibit no more douchal display than the highly noxious revelation of their well-defined, vaguely lobsterian, vaguely crustacean, douche-abs.

Abacrabs are sea creatures of taint—a potent mixture of ancient sea-faring scrotundae dating back millions of years. Yet they are also one of the hardest of the latter-day 'bags to spot, as revelation of their true nature can be rare. Spotting an Abacrab in the wild long enough to capture in picture form is an infrequent occurrence and should be celebrated. By throwing your gin and tonica at them.

But be careful. Abacrab's Alien face–hugger six-pack abs might jump out and implant an alien egg in your stomach. They're alive and strangely hypnotic, like a swirling *Twilight Zone* spiral of scrotal wankosity.

THE POUCH 'BAG

Most displays of shirtless douchebaggery involve a variety of ab revelations, as evidenced by the Abacrab. Ab revelation communicates douchal masculinity by gesturing toward his exposed abs and crying, "Woo!" and "Yeah, boyee!" This male peacocking serves as a primal mating call to summon the boobies. The 'bag hopes he can impress the hottie by revealing his superior muscular detail. And the hottie will often respond with approving cries of "Woo!!"

However, a category of ab display separate and distinct from the Abacrab is what scrotologists term the Pouch 'Bag. This shirtless Pouch 'Bag reveals one- or two-pack abs—a saggy, perhaps once Abacrab-level ab set now reduced to the inevitable gravitational pull of saggy sag. The Pouch 'Bag's sag combines with bling to cauterize infected wounds with the sheer force of scrotebaggery. As such, it is perhaps even more potent than its rock-stomached crustacean cousin.

Meanwhile, Russian Minx Cutie looks for a way to smuggle the microfilm out. I suggest planting it on the cabana boy.

DOUCHE MCCLEVERSHIRT

One of the quickest ways to tag a semi-benign, but still fully-formed, douchescrote is by noticing his clever shirt.

While a shirt with a silly, usually crude slogan does not automatically qualify a dude for douche status, it certainly hints at douchal blight. But while there is significant overlap with some of the other sections of standard douchebaggery, we should still give Douche McClevershirt his own category.

It is fairly straightforward to figure out exactly when a clever T-shirt crosses over from mildly annoying urban gnat into a true douche. Classification is made on the basis of the following determination: If you need a clever T-shirt to seem like you have a personality, the actual subtext of the T-shirt is that you have no personality.

But Douche McClevershirts can only achieve 'bag status when in the presence of a Kelly from Arizona State, as pictured here. The type who makes you want to yell, "GO HOME TEAM MASCOT!!" in the hopes she'll get stupid drunk with you at the tailgate party. At which point you would slobber on her shoes like a hungry sheepdog and play Geddy Lee drum solos on her butt with licorice.

THE HIPPIEBAG

Hippiebags invoke the memories of Spin Doctors-playing, mid-1990s, hackey-sack and Ultimate Frisbee–filled summers. These Fratdouches disguise themselves with long hair and scruff in the hopes that a couple of sexually frustrated Sarah Lawrence girls might want to do lemon drop shots, make out with each other, and strip to a Phish bootleg.

The Hippiebag is one of the rarest of douche categories, as the hippie look has grown increasingly unpopular among the Woo-Hotties persuaded by the dark douchal arts. This cultural reorientation toward the greased-up metro überdouche has had a diminishing effect on Hippiebag manifestation. Hotties are trading in the scruff for grease.

But in some circles, and I'm looking at you Bennington University, the unshaven Hippiebag look is still a go-to oblique strategy to gain the attention of the lunchable leg hotness, pictured here.

The colliding impossibilities of this hot little candy corn and this taco o'douche personifies the essence of the Hippiebag strategy, and how a trained 'bag hunter can spot one in action.

THE YUPPIEBAG

Yuppiebags are designer-brand oil. They are hidden ur-grease.

Working day jobs on Wall Street, they're your average broker—charming, normal, and relatively friendly. But at night, the Yuppiebag flips into his party persona. He oils up his forehead and attempts to charm cute suburban hotties like an outbreak of viral skeeze. In this way, the Yuppiebag operates like a Jeckyl and Hyde of sleazy dual identity.

Observe Yuppiebag's classic lean in and head-butt into bouncy Miss Long Island Iced Tea. She remains remarkably oblivious to the fact she's standing next to a Yupscrote.

Yuppiebags exist at the low end of the annoyance spectrum of the douche hierarchy. Yet they are still best avoided by crossing the street before coming into close proximity. Not because Yuppiebags are scary or threatening. They're about as dangerous as a Chihuahua on No-Doze. But Yuppiebags display Wall Street ooze so prominently that you could get smeared without even realizing it. As such, approach a Yuppiebag with caution.

THE GARDEN GNOME

There is little that needs to be said about the Garden Gnome branch of douchebagology. Identifying him correctly is obvious simply from witnessing one in action. Often furry and feral, Garden Gnomes venture far from traditional douchebaggery, yet they are still scrotey and rank. They rarely rise to the higher levels of the douche hierarchy, and instead seem content to maintain second-tier 'bag status.

A Garden Gnome's facial piercings are the key giveaway. They cause surrealist art to spontaneously become drenched in blue paint and Taoist monks to silently scream in protest. Their Opie hair kills mosquitoes and euthanizes the African jaguarundi. Their kung-fu grip on hotties melts Vermont cheddar cheese and cures headaches.

To spot a Garden Gnome in action, a 'bag hunter must look for the less obvious signs. But the douchitude is plain to see, once one knows what to look for. The Garden Gnome is everything that's rotten in Denmark. Latina Hott is everything that's golden in Guadalcanal.

THE ÜBERMENSCHBAG

The nineteenth-century German philosopher Friedrich Nietzsche famously wrote about the state when an individual moves beyond societally imposed notions of good and evil and ascends to a place of pure überdouche. This means he must mack on the bottle blondes outside of socially defined cultural parameters.

It is a state that Nietzsche describes as *the Übermenschbag*.

Rare is the individual who can reach such a lofty state of douchewankery purely through having awareness of what is outside the cultural latticework of societal imposition. But some do. Like Stingbag, pictured here in his waxen, android state.

Do douchebags dream of electric sheep? Perhaps we'll never know. But while the übermenschbag attempts to operate outside of societal norms, his douchebaggery is still classifiable. As such, it can be mocked accordingly. By laughing at the shiny head.

THE POWERBAR 'BAG

This skinny ball of generi-douche is best described as a blended energy drink of scrotal fusion. He's the douche fruit blend on the menu at Jamba Juice, right between Berry Protein and Guava Energy.

Add a free Frosted Hair Boost, and it's $4.95 well spent.

Powerbar 'Bags are those vaguely trendy, yet entirely innocuous, categories of douchescrote. Like the health food and smoothie craze, they taste vaguely of real douche, yet they leave you slightly unfulfilled, hungry. A 'bag snack between 'bag meals: a Powerbar 'Bag.

Powerbar 'Bags are often spotted with Scandinavian Former Nun Teacher Hotties—the type who coldly dismiss you from class and scold you for wearing improper dress by rapping your knuckles with a ruler. Which would excite you in vastly inappropriate ways.

CRO 'BAGNON

The Cro 'Bagnon is neither muscle douche nor Bouncerbag. He's located in an ambiguous nexus between actual douchery and surreal cartoonish spectacle.

Cro 'Bagnon is neither quite human, nor quite Hulk. Therefore, Cro 'Bagnon is only partial 'bag. One must allow for his uniqueness and get the hell out of the way before he snaps your femur bone like a Twix bar.

However ambiguous his placement is between the douchological spectrum and Saturday-morning Transformers cartoons, we can generally locate Cro 'Bagnon as a cross between Lou Ferrigno and a crate filled with lumpy oranges.

I mean, look at that head.

It's crazy big. Mack-truck big. Just contemplating its hyper-reality spectacle is enough to make me sucker punch a dwarf and ask for change.

PRINCE ASSPIAN

The metrosexual dandy is not a recent development in douche hierarchy.

This elaborate example of male spectacle has been around since at least the mid-1800s in Europe, when young factory workers would dress up in elaborate Victorian garb in an attempt to woo as many proletariat bar wenches as possible.

This traditional douche maneuver exists today in the form of the modern-day dandybag, or what we'll term the Prince Asspian. Prince Asspian douchewanks adopt the codes of European aristocracy to paint a portrait of mythic lore. Their fantastical garb evokes a land where dragons are slain and noble lords ride to the rescue of slutty club-going hotties with wonderfully curved hindquarters.

To complete this illusion, Prince Asspians adopt a vague European accent and elaborately feminized hairstyle. The point of this is for the Asspian to code himself outside the parameters of the current fashion trends and styles, which is itself an inverted form of trendy douche aesthetic. It's the non-douche douche maneuver.

While Prince Asspians often imply significant trust-fund financial reserves, this is usually a ruse. By day the average Prince Asspian goes by the name of Teddy and is a cashier at the local Denny's, where they're happy to deliver your Grand Slam Breakfast with elaborate Victorian flourish in the hopes you'll tip closer to twenty percent. Which you won't. Because he's a tool.

THE DADABAG

Think of this hottie/douchey coupling as a form of modern art. It varies greatly from standard douchebaggery, operating on the fringes of the avant-'bag.

DaDaBag has the anti-aesthetic revulsion of reactionary discourse. His cap, orange tie, and ginormous 'stache echo the surrealist masterpieces of Dali and Ernst. He confuses and astounds with his illogical douchtundae.

Stare at him long enough and he becomes abstract, out of time, and removed from all reality.

Together, DaDaBag and DaDa Hott produce a surreal image that Marcel Douchamp would stick on a bicycle wheel and call *Douche Wheel*. Something Buñuel, Man Ray, and Stieglitz would celebrate on the Left Bank while sipping absinthe and hitting on a fifteen-year-old peasant girl named Monique.

THE CACTUSBAG

Cactusbags are a crucial subsection of the douchological spectrum in that they have a wide range of manifestations and variations.

Note the large, firm desert follicles protruding from the base of the skull. These spiky desert hairs are adept at holding water and surviving disparate climate temperatures and predatory attacks.

Cactusbags are known to cohabitate with the purest of sexy hotness, as seen here with Power Hottie. She reminds me of all that is worthwhile about attending school on an army base in the Pacific Rim. Sure, I got a crap education, drank a lot of sake, and bid my time before returning stateside. But at least you got the occasional butt bongo cameo with Asian perfection and the State Schoolettes. It gave me something to remember fondly before joining up with the Hong Kong Cavaliers in the battle against the Red Lectroids from Planet 10.

THE OLDBAG

Creepy Oldbags are the one exception in douche classification in that they tend to gain a sort of anti-hero popularity. When a douche is young, utterly scroterific, and gang-tackling the hotties, he's a rank piece of detritus floating in a choad sea.

But once that same 'bag passes forty and is still out there tackling the hott with awkward headlocks, he becomes like a Grieco Billy the Kid. A folk hero. A rebel douche. He acquires a form of legendary heroism simply for keeping his saggy scrotundae in the game.

As such, we must invert our normal mocking and give it up to Oldie here. Busting the sexy see-through shirt and stylin' hubcap necklace, the Oldbag somehow forces a grudging respect. It's like a stroke victim finally being able to swallow a spoonful of pudding. Sure, it's still sad. But, in its own way, it's damn impressive.

TAGGING THE 'BAGLINGS: HOW TO SPOT STAGE-1 SCROTERY

NOW THAT WE'VE categorized the broad spectrum of douchitude, we need to take a step back and consider the pre-douche. We must examine the early warning signs of the Stage-1 scrotundae, the toe-dipping 'bagling.

Just as an early morning dew-covered forsythia unfolds slowly in the dawn, testing its stamen against the crisp breeze, a young douche awkwardly tests his tentative scrotewank. And just as every rose has its thorn, every 'bagling sings a sad, sad song.

Now that we have seen a full douche, we are better tuned to react to the early warning signs. By parsing these primitive stages of the developing 'bagling, we can better anticipate, and thus mock, any aspiring pud who yearns to douche with impunity. This will also help to alert any developing hotties who are inadvertently supporting such choadal growth by applauding their young douchuous counterparts.

So how do we identify the covert signs of emerging scrote?

Some call it ESP. Others call it a rash on my sack that needs medical attention. But most call it the Sixth Scrote: the mystical art of predicting future douchebaggery based on scrotal sensation.

the male genitalia. First written about in Jacques Lacan's famous treatise, *The Four Fundamental States of Scrotey Douchewankery,* it is an important and emerging field of douchal study.

This classification process uses scrotal vibration as its central methodology—a deep-rooted, almost otherworldly response located in the scrotum of the witness of hottie/douchey commingling. With accurate predictive powers located somewhere between Mistress Cleo, Kreskin, and *Harry Potter and the Grease on the Nutsack,* the scrotum is able to sense early warning douchebaggery with remarkable clarity and focus.

For female 'bag hunters, lacking scrotum does not prevent the ability to utilize the Sixth Scrote. For it does not require an actual scrotum, only a metaphorical pouch. It is a projection of the Self within the simulacrum of the hottie/douche image being observed. Simply stare at the following pictures of early 'baglings and choadbugs, and measure your reaction.

If you feel a scrotological vibration, you are learning how to suss out the early 'bag within his not yet fully-formed state of pre-douche. Once you've fine-tuned your scrotological sixth sense, you will be better equipped to prevent future development from spreading.

So let all our scrotums, real and metaphorical, begin vibrating in harmonic response. For these are the categories of early douchosity/hottie development in all their primitive, budding forms.

THE 'BAGLING

'Baglings, sometimes known as Budding 'Bags, are the most basic and prevalent category of early 'bag identification.

'Baglings begin to show signs of douche aptitude anywhere from freshman year of high school through their mid-twenties, when their lives rapidly decay thanks to temp jobs and studio apartments.

In the 'bagling phase, collars begin to pop, albeit slightly and hesitantly. Caps begin to tilt, but only in three- or four-degree angles. Douche head-

bands begin to sprout from the forehead like cloth elephantitis of the skull. Classic 'bag gestures like the Douche Ab Reveal (*left*) emerge tentatively.

To spot a 'bagling, one must first look for a group social situation. 'Baglings usually begin to practice communicative douchosity in the presence of the emerging hottie, or what gender theorists term Pre-Hotts. Pre-Hotts encourage douchal growth through positive reinforcement.

An example of this would be the Pre-Hott responding to a 'bagling's early efforts with a comment like, "Kevin, you look smokin'!" or "Ha-ha, you're such a playah, Dylan!"

While extensive studies have yet to be completed, the general conversion rate from 'bagling to full douche is estimated somewhere between 60 and 70 percent.

As such, mocking 'baglings becomes imperative. Think of it as a form of cultural shock therapy. By relentlessly teasing the 'bagling until he is shamed into submission, short-term behavior modification can be achieved through the crippling cruelty of social disgrace and humiliation. Or what I refer to affectionately as, "The Way Dad Raised Me."

Sure, it leaves long lasting scars, and drove me to drink and extensive therapy.

But it works. It really works.

At least I think it works.

HOWDY DOUCHEY

Like the famous 1950s wooden puppet that bears its name, Howdy Douchey 'bags don't have to do much to achieve 'bagling status. Their blank facial expressions and vaguely plastic-like shiny foreheads do most of the work for them.

However, while Howdy Doucheys appear generally harmless and un-threatening, they achieve a level of 'bagling status due to their single-minded mission statement. They are determined to occupy space with hotties long enough to have the moment captured in digital photographic form.

Only by capturing the hott in pic form proximity, can the Howdy Douchey prove his scrotey self-worth to his friends back home and achieve his mythical street cred. Such photography is usually accompanied by im-probable tales involving such claims as, "She wanted me, dude."

No, Howdy Douchey. No, she did not.

Howdy Doucheys are just starting down the oily path of grease, but like the other Stage-1 'baglings, their ability to morph into full-blown scrote is a potent one. Given the right conditions, Howdy Doucheys are only a few years away from full-on tatted-out, faux-hawk, scroteshow presentational überdouchosity.

As to Howdy Douchey's hotties pictured here, they will likely make your funny pants go "Yayyy!!" along with the kids on the short bus. The perfect brunette in yellow bespeaks a thousand New England swans quacking har-monic melodies on a bright blue moonlit New Hampshire lake. She inspires dreams of flight betwixt satin cumulous clouds that transform maple trees into curvy hills of marshmallow.

THE SKANKNUT

The Skanknut is a catch-all category for the rare and blazing douche apparition. Like Halley's Comet. Or your freshman-year roommate finally getting some.

While the Skanknut may come flying out of nowhere to dazzle the pros and amaze onlookers with his boobal grabbing and chest reveal, he retains lower level 'bag status because of the inconsistency of his game.

Will the Skanknut stay on a douche roll? Or will his wank disappear as quickly as it surfaced?

This uncertainty confines the Skanknut to a douche hybrid. Skanknuts can break either way along the douche/non-douche spectrum. But their risk factor for development into mature scrotal blister remains high enough that they merit monitoring.

FURRY-MAN

Beware the Furry-man.

Like a legend told at campfire sites by Maori tribal elders, the story of the Furry-man is as old as the hills, and as greasy as the Grieco.

No one knows where Furry-man lives. Or if he's even real. They only know of his legendary powers that include craptastic dance-floor, hairy-chested suckitude.

Furry-men can be hard to spot, as the display of their furriness may be infrequent. Similar to the Skanknut, these unformed 'baglings often teeter into normalcy for long periods of time, before betraying their douchal tendencies.

It is unwise for Furry-man to choose not to manscape his chest sweater. Electric clippers can play an important role in hiding an urban tribal legend, as well as helping the rest of us keep down our lunch. Furry-man is not a pure douche, as hair sweaters alone can't qualify one as true 'bag. But they warrant 'bagling status for their occasional flashing of chest forest.

THE SOPHOMORE 'BAG

The sophomore-year choadbag is one of the more celebrated of the early scrotological sub-genres. And by celebrated, I mean laughed at by his classmates, who didn't invite him to their party.

Sophomore 'Bags are more developed than Skanknuts or 'baglings, but not quite ready to assume the mantle of accomplished professional douche. Note the oversized red-satin shirt and horns 'bag hand gesture. Those gestures inform the budding douche essence of this Sophomore 'Bag, celebrating his second year in college by crawling out of his gelled-up cocoon and taking his first awkward steps into a larger douchiverse.

Sophomore 'Bags haunt coed dorms and shared kitchen areas like the collegiate version of Marley's Ghost. They rattle their douche chains, these Ghosts of Douchemas Future, predicting the day when they're in their late thirties, making 80K as mid-level analysts, and hitting up the Applebees bars every night to unsuccessfully mack on some honeys.

Sophomore 'Bags display an innate ability to pull collegiate hotts who know not yet the value of their hotness. She is iced banana college hottie sexiness with a dash of Copenhagen. Given the chance, you would nibble her earlobes softly and whisper the ingredients off a package of Ho Hos with all the sexiness you could muster—*wheat gluten . . . sodium caseinate . . . sorbic acid*—until she tells you to get out of her dorm room or calls the R.A. And you leave quietly.

THE "HE'S MY BEST FRIEND" 'BAG

Best Friend 'Baglings are deceptively clever in their oblique approach to the nubile college hott.

They smile. Their faces only faintly glow of douche grease. Their bling is muted. Their hand gestures minimal.

But do not underestimate the lurking scrotewankery.

Best Friend 'Baglings hide their true douchuousness in the shadows. They wait for the perfect drunken moment of pounce, hoping that the hottie's standards have dropped well below that of most of outer Long Island. Somewhere between Dix Hills and Montauk.

The hotties always know. They intuit the lurking pouncery of Best Friend 'Bagling. And it's coming. Oh, yes. It's most certainly coming. I give it two hours, four lemon drop shots, and one extended conversation about how majoring in pre-med is "like, totally off the hook."

THIRD-EYE 'BAG

Mystical Hindu gurus believe that if you pray and meditate long enough, enlightenment can be attained through visions that come to the third eye, located inside the center area of the forehead. This place is a location for deep spiritual insight, and the nexus point of higher consciousness.

The douche corollary to this philosophy is, of course, the third eyebrow, located as a fungal growth on the lower lip. Otherwise known as *chin pubes*.

Third Eye 'Bags are not douchey enough for us to confer full-fledged

douche status on them, and as such, we must demarcate them only as indicators of 'baglings. In the pic featured here, the third eye demonstrates deep introspection. And by introspection, I mean Living Like an Angel and Dying Like a Devil. Which is deep.

This sultry vixen's top looks like it got into a car wreck with a third-grade art project. However, she could be covered by earthworms dipped in arsenic and I'd still watch a sixteen-hour marathon of commercial-free *7th Heaven* episodes from 1997 just for the chance to sniff her kitchen oven mitts.

THE CHINBAG

We've established facial 'bag classifications as diverse as the Tonguebag, the Kissy Lips, and, of course, the Douche Face. But Chinbags occupy a strange sort of nether-region of 'bag classification. Like a Michael Jackson–vitiligo inspired Rorschach blot, it's ambiguous, confusing, and smells vaguely like halibut.

If we classify douchebaggery according to performativity, it is perhaps unfair to lump Chinbags into their own category. Unlike the douche face, the 'bag hand gesture, or the tongue-scrote, a chinbag cannot control the doucheyness of his jawline. It is there from birth.

We must factor in ancillary evidence, like, in the example provided here, the wispy blond-tipped fauxhawk. Meanwhile, this hottie clings with succulent shoulder-of-lamb-and-mint-jelly tenderness. Her lightly powdered cheekbones sing harmonic twelve-tone compositions performed by the Kronos Quartet. In my pants.

She reminds me of my seventh-grade girlfriend all grown up. Not in my pants.

Because why would my seventh-grade girlfriend be in my pants?
Come on now.

CHAPTER 7

THE STAGE-4 ÜBERBAG: WHEN DOUCHEBAGGERY KILLS

FROM 'BAGLINGS we now move to the other end of the douche spectrum: the Stage-4 Überbag. The Power Douche. Scrotimus Prime.

These are the rarified categories of the überdouche. The Stage-4 urscrotes from which even the strongest of hotties cannot recover. These are the source douches from which extended exposure of boob hott will result only in tragic Bleeth nightmares. They must be categorized.

And by categorized I mean mocked.

It takes a special level of oiled-up, hyper-sphincter consciousness to reach the hallowed and rarified plateau of the überdouche. It is a triumph of choad. A wealth of wigga. A transcendence of tribal tatt.

Those legendary few who raise their game to this level eclipse the mere skeezy, fratbag, and low-level amateur douchology involving tongue and hand gesturing. For these enlightened scrotepuddles, a physical gesture is simply unnecessary. Their leptons, muons, electrons, and hairy chin fungus all vibrate with transcendent douchal harmonic oscillation.

For they have reached what I like to term *Douche Nirvana*.

Only by reaching this state of douche ascendance do the überchoads

find fulfillment. Spiritual justification located within the sexual congress of the hottie they have ensnared.

Featuring body lotions of the soul, barbed wire tatts of spiritual mani-festation, and the requisite sexy Miami Beach chiquitas by their side, their embodiment conveys a cumulative spectacle that can be described only as amplified visual overload.

Only by creating a pure and an uncut Douche Spectacle can their spiritual seagull open his enlightened wings and fly off into the setting sun of karmic awakening and electric Kool-Aid.

A setting sun, that is, of poo.

THE CHAOS THEORY 'BAG

Somewhere in China, a butterfly flaps its wings. At the exact moment when that butterfly flaps its wings, halfway around the world, an oiled-up douchescrote unleashes a primal scream and makes a really, really silly 'bag hand gesture.

It is Chaos Theory 'Bag. The butterfly and the scrote are connected. Ten-dimensional quantum mechanisms we can barely comprehend bind their energies together like some giant Silly String of scrotological douche mud. A metaphorical jelly doughnut as vast as the universe.

A douchal gravity pull that is so strong that hotties swirl around like confetti in a bathtub. Not that I've seen swirling confetti in a bathtub. At least not since my last appendix operation.

Chaos Theory 'Bag can exist only in the presence of a Curly Sue Hott. The type who cuts a lithe, sultry, cherry Popsicle flavor on the dance floor. The downtown–New York, used-to-be-a-model hott. The kind you take to wine-tasting events on Ludlow Street before heading to her studio apartment on Avenue C.

Only in the presence of such hott can Chaos Theory 'Bag alter the path of butterflies through sheer quantum douchery.

LAST OF THE MOHAWKANS

The Last of the Mohawkans is that rockstar wannabe, music major überpud who takes things to an extreme level of shaved-headed ballsackery. And, as with all the Stage-4 choads, his hottie is as juicy as his head is melon fungus.

Mohawkans are Punkbags taken to the next level of scrotological wank. As a fan of punk, I'd be loath to dismiss the mohawk as solely the province of modern male performative douchebaggery. Yet, at the same time, this ain't 1977. Joey Ramone is dead, Johnny Rotten is a grumpy old man, and CBGB's T-shirts are now sold at Wal-Mart.

This leaves us with one conclusion: The club-going Mohawkan is auto-douche.

This pic launched the Peloponnesian War. Its digitized pixilated 1s and 0s punched a Nigerian poet named Umbutu in the buttocks. Which is just mean. Because Umbutu is a good guy.

As with every Stage-4 überdouche, Mohawkan's hott is fantastic. I would worship her used towels discarded after forty sweaty minutes on the Stairmaster 2000. I would bake chocolate truffles and feed them to her one by one while playing yoga meditation music on Zamfir's pan flute. Then I would rub her feet with talcum powder until she got bored and asked for my credit card to hit Loehmann's.

Which I would gladly give up.

Because Loehmann's is having a sale.

THE "THERE-IS-NO-GOD" 'BAG

Theologists and philosophers have long debated whether there is a deity that watches over us. "There-Is-No-God" überbags answer this query with powerful finality.

No. There is no God.

No God would allow such toolsheds to occupy the same air space as this sexy little vixen. No divine power could possibly allow two complete and utter beef jerkies in the presence of a sweet slice of key lime pie.

Witnessing a "There-Is-No-God" 'Bag in person is cause for sober contemplation and humble reflection. It requires us to pause in awe at a vast and epic universe, of which we know so little, yet is so damn douchey. It makes us bow our heads as we comprehend the irrefutable settling of this age-old metaphysical question—the profoundly tragic realization of our isolated meaningless genetic happenstance.

Or we can just stare at this chick's fantastic tatas.

THE DHARMA 'BAG

Proving that even the pudgiest choad can attract hotties with space and time–bending gravitational pull, the Dharma 'Bag's Zen transcendence remains inspirational. And by inspirational, I mean spewy.

Dharma 'Bags are identified by their use of an almost spiritual scrotal transcendence to cause hotties to swarm to their earthly manifestations. They are the mutant spawn of 1950s beatnik wanderlust by way of Eastern mysticism and Miami Beach grease.

The Dharma 'Bag reeks of transcendent spitwater douchosity. All while Blue-eyed Doe glances at us mockingly, her eyes probing us with that most basic of questions: "Are you spiritual enough to fondle my can-cans?"

Were it so, Blue-eyed Doe. Were it so.

It is important to delineate the Dharma 'Bag's überdouchosity from the standard Buddhabag. While both feature East Asian douche-fusion, they are not the same. Dharma 'Bag teaches the Four Douchey Truths and offers us the Eightfold Path of Scrote. As such, he is the gateway to douche mastery.

Buddhabags simply look like Buddha.

THE VELVEETA 'BAG

One of the most potent of all the überbags is the processed American cheese of nuclear douchosity. That pale, curdled milk packaged and sold as pure douchal product: the Velveeta 'Bag.

I blame the atrocity of Velveeta douchitude on men's fashion magazines. Somewhere between the airbrushed pages of glossy male model preening, and the echo effect of wannabes trying to emulate the poses, lies Velveetic überdouche. This male spectacle is competing with his hottie, vying for our attention with the musically dissonant wrongness of post-classical composition.

Velveeta 'Bags are the powerful alpha douche of every club scene, and rarely does more than one occupy a dance floor at any given time. They seek to emulate the fashion-metro-model-gone-club-promoter. Projecting ambiguous sexuality, they disarm the hottie to enable a more effective pounce. But the hott is not their ultimate goal. They preen and pose for pictures, and require the spectacle of their presence to receive attention at all times. Only then does a Velveeta 'Bag feel accomplished.

A common reaction upon witnessing a Velveeta 'Bag in person is to take out any frustrations by subsequently kicking young British street urchins in the shins.

Which is mean.

Because they just want some more porridge.

THE DOUCHE VORTEX

Not to be confused with the Chaos Theory 'Bag, this vortex of nodal douchedom represents a key point on the quantum douche axis. It's a douche singularity, a black hole of scrotal 'baggery.

Refracting light and bending gravity itself, this douche vortex registers on Richter scales in Osaka and neutrino oscillation detectors in the southern region of Istanbul (not Constantinople).

It is that powerful.

Physicists are still debating whether Douche Pull factors of (a)XiS>T(ag) outweigh the bl/i(ng) {s(cr) x O(t)=e} methodology.

What scientists have been able to determine is that I would gather twigs, string, and bark and build a nest for the summer down in the boobal regions of silky phantasmagorical dreamland. Then I would awaken, and ask for a glass of milk. And a Fig Newton.

Because her boobies make Schrödinger's Cat choose life.

THE TATTBAG

There is a key ruling in überbag classification. Tats that make up more than 40 percent of the chestal region and do not earn money next to the Bearded Lady on Coney Island are automatic überdouche. Stage-4. Call the fire department to hose down the scrote. For he is festering.

Tattbags can be excused in certain instances, such as official rockstardom or large record deals. There is a distinct correlation between successful talent and forgiveness of visual überdouchosity. However, one must separate the wheatbags from the chaffbags, the successful rockdouche from the Stage-4 poser.

In the Tattbag example pictured here, the only excuse is a #1 hit within the last three years. Otherwise, the desire to shave his faux-hawk nest with a shank spoon found in the gravel outside San Quentin, then sing medieval Gregorian chants with a hip-hop beat until hottie is forced to pat one's bottom with melted candy corn residue, is a reasonable reaction. For he is very, very smelly.

XENU

Few aspiring 'bags are able to reach an alien warlord state of pure metaphysical douchitude.

Enter, Xenu.

He has attained that rare and exclusive peak level of greasy clarity, after spending tens of thousands of dollars on auditing classes in a compound off Hollywood Boulevard. And a three-week series of treatments at Sunset Tan.

Like the ancient and mythic warlord of 1960s pop psychobabble from whence they take their name, Xenu douches exist in a state of pure hyper science-fiction religious hack-job clarity. They remain in absolute douchethink: a rarified consciousness of hyper-intense sleaze. They write lousy sci-fi books just for the chance to romance MTV hottie while explaining human behavior using alien creature metaphors and warmed over Freud.

Xenu is the highest point of the Stage-4 ubërbag. He is Source Douche Clarity itself. As such, he is to be feared as much as mocked. Only the most experienced of 'bag hunters can dare take on a Xenu. Until your training is complete, it is best to turn tail and run should you find yourself in one's presence.

CHAPTER 8

THE FOUR STAGES
OF BLEETH

WHEN RICHARD GRIECO, the Originary Source Douche himself, first appeared on the scene in *21 Jump Street* in the late 1980s, his powers of scrotal radiation hadn't yet reached terminal capacity. Even after Fair Maiden Bleeth dated the Grieco during her *Baywatch* days in the mid-1990s, it took a number of years of direct exposure to Douchosity before she collapsed into a tragic douchebaguette.

What we can learn from that hottie/douchey legend is that Bleething is not instantaneous. It takes time. Thus, it is important to note that the hottie descent into female douchebaggery must be tracked according to key stages of scrotal decay.

There are four main stages of douchebaguette that occur when a cute ball of boob is exposed to rank überscrote. To descend to each subsequent level of douchebaguette, the hottie must be exposed to a 'bag over a length of time that allows her to absorb the bling, facial sneers, and hand gestures projected onto her by the scrotal emanation of the male's radiant douchosity.

As with any delicate flower in the presence of so violent a wank-flame, decay is inevitable. But it is not instantaneous.

This is good news. It tells us that a cutie's exposure, caught quickly enough, can be reversed. But the flip side is grim. Like with any form of radiation, too much exposure and a hottie with perfect thighs that I would suckle for a fortnight is lost forever.

She becomes irredeemably and irreversibly Bleethed.

STAGE 1: THE INNOCENT

The Stage-1 Bleeth is perhaps the easiest to identify. With an Ivory Snow face, and a clavicle I'd nibble on with tartar sauce and lemon, the Stage-1 hottie is a young, perky girl of happy disposition.

She has yet to taste from the dark, alluring cesspool of douchebaggery. As such, she is to be celebrated. If she lives in your neighborhood, you should crouch awkwardly outside her bedroom window at 2 a.m. Until she calls the police. It's the only way to show proper appreciation.

There are no signs of Bleeth in a Stage-1 hottie. Even in the frozen pixilated presence of an Abacrab pud, she retains an angelic presence, untouched by Douche Virus.

The Stage-1 Bleeths are those innocents we project as our redeeming angel. The ones we seek out to take care of us, to feed us and pamper our bottoms and bring over their bisexual best friend every so often.

They are what I like to call *antibihotics*. Antibihotics can cure any infection of the soul. Any festering sore on the psyche. Simply by being. By existing as fried oyster Zen hottitude. As Om-presence boobarific polished shine.

I would wade through a sea of piranhas in the rivers of Africa while carrying a stack of iron maidens, juggling ostrich eggs, gargling a double shot of Listerine and lighter fluid, and humming the theme to *Rawhide* merely for the pleasure of firing off organic cucumber fireworks at the base of a forty-foot shrine made of bamboo shoots and plantains, just to pay tribute to a Stage-1 Bleeth's innocence.

I would set sail to the Pacific on a small Hong Kong junk with only my cunning and a small Nepalese slave boy to survive just for the chance to knead a Stage-1 Bleeth's unwashed sundress into a tub of Jell-O mixed with distilled Utah moonshine.

These are the dream myths that only a Stage-1 Bleeth can inspire.

STAGE 2: THE GUM SNAPPER

Observing the exact moment when an innocent, young, Stage-1 hottie begins to take on the early form signs of Douche Infection can be challenging. Douchey hand gestures and ridiculously large sunglasses are just beginning to sprout from the formerly innocent hottie's inner 'bag.

Stage-2 Bleeths can be classified based on when they exhibit the vaguest hint of scrotewankery, or the first scrunchy signs of a douche face. They wear minimal, but annoying, hip-hop bling and demonstrate 'Bag Hand Gesture #194. They are still relatively unpolluted, even in close proximity to sweat-stained rocker douches. But grease infection has clearly and unambiguously taken root. You will know that Stage-2 has been reached when a hottie's gestures attract dudes who resemble fetid kangaroo poo.

Stage-2 hotties are still redeemable. Slightly scrotey, true, but still with the potential to reform and recover their formerly innocent, boobalicious, and lunchable-leg innocence.

The Stage-2 Bleeth is also known as the Hottie on the Cusp. These are the ones to reach out and fondle in inappropriate ways. For therein lies the hope for our collective societal future.

So while the Stage-2 Bleeth demonstrates some signs of douchebaggery, they can still be saved. And by saved, I mean that we would read her Longfellow by flashlight while rubbing her calves with baking powder and suckling on her shoulder like a hungry rain forest Madagascar leech.

STAGE 3: THE BAGUETTE

It is extremely difficult to pinpoint exactly when a Bleeth crosses the event horizon from a still innocent Stage-1 or semi-polluted Stage-2, in which hopes of redemption are still viable, into Stages 3 and 4 of douchebaguette-level apostasy.

As a general guiding principle, this crossing over occurs somewhere between the moment of early ginormous sunglasses growth and the sprouting of 'baguette hand gestures—and reaches a crisis state with the combo smug pout and the douchechoad embrace maneuver.

But how do we quantify exactly when this takes place? What is the exact moment when a hottie has become so tainted through overwhelming exposure to radioactive isodouche that she becomes Bleethed?

Unfortunately, the answer to this deep metascrotal question is that there is no precise answer.

We can locate the general area of hottie descent, but we can never precisely pinpoint that exact moment when the hottie becomes lost to the dark ways of Bleeth. We will never know when she is unredeemable, never to return from the land of greasy foreheads, douchey dog tags, and unbuttoned shirts.

This ambiguity may seem to limit us. Without knowledge of a clear dividing line, how do we know when to attempt to de-Bleeth a hottie and when to abandon hope because she is lost forever? The answer is that we don't.

But within this vagary, we find hope. So long as we believe a hottie can be saved from an oily douchescrote, there is that glimmer of utopian ideal that sustains us. And by utopian ideal, I mean boobs.

This ambiguity of taxonomical classification leads us, perhaps paradoxically, toward one simple, but incontrovertible, fact. I would fondle baby raccoons dressed in burkas just for the chance to filter tea through her stockings and make a Hott Toddy.

STAGE 4: THE BLEETH

So what happens when the Grieco Virus reaches a terminal state of infection? When the Bleeth has journeyed well past any possible point of no return?

Ah, I say. Aha.

To answer this question, we must first confront the mystical Double 'Bag Head. Few have glimpsed this state of spiritual hybridity—when hottie/douchey couples reach a terminal nexus of douchebaguousness so dark and scrotey, not even Tag Bodyshot Clouds can escape its gravitational pull. These Choads and Bleeths have fused into one nuclear state known as the *douchetron*.

Boobies are everywhere. But the innocence is long lost. These are the Stage-4 Bleeths. Those curvy, fleshy hotties so corrupted by extended scrotal presence, they may never again regain their purity.

But this realization brings with it a vexing contradiction. The involuntary reaction from even the most jaded 'bag hunter is: "But the hotties are still hott!"

Yes. Yes they are.

And herein lies the profound philosophical key to understanding the Bleething process. Even in those most extreme of the Stage-4 Bleeths, douchebaguette and desire are not mutually exclusive.

This means that the Stage-4 Bleeth, while tragic, does not preclude the maintaining of a desire to explore the Holy Cleavite with the primal fascina-

tion of a shrieking rhesus monkey grabbing Play-Doh. Such base instincts remain, even as they face the intellectual awareness of unrecoverable infection.

In short, you realize they're douched-out Bleeths. But you still want to do naughty things to their underdress. This is OK.

This state of simultaneous desire and revulsion toward the presence of a Stage-4 Bleeth hottie is referred to as the Douchadox. The 'bag hunter is both aroused and repelled.

Only by accepting the apparent contradiction of the Douchadox can one classify a Stage-4 Bleether during examination. And by examination I mean boobie examination. And by boobie examination, I mean staring longingly at those marshmallow pillows while drooling like a quadriplegic on Benzedrine.

PART 3:

THE ROAD TO
RECOVERY:
DOUCHE
DE-DOUCHIFICATION

We have now covered all the major categories of 'Bag and Bleeth, Choad and Boob, curvy, powdered thigh and smelly-ass cesspool. We have critically examined every permutation, sociological mutation, and scatological poo nation, to the point where you, the reader, may realize that either you or someone you love is a douche.

So now what?

You're worried. You've learned that 'baggery is a path of cumulative totality that ends only in disaster. And now you want to change. You want to reform your douchey/hottie commingling ways and find your way back to the light of un-'bag. Normalcy. A real-world authenticity where collars stay down and specialty male body perfumes do not present themselves as viable personal hygiene products.

Good news. This is your chance.

For 'bags, the following program is a step-by-step road to recovery to regain the humanity you lost in a sea of bling, spiky cactus hair, and puke-worthy sunglasses.

For the hotties, it's a journey you can take to help purge your douche-counterpart's oily-infected psyche.

The road will be a long and painful one. But it is well worth undertaking.

If you're a moderate-level douche, a Stage-2/3 'tweener who

hasn't yet taken the full plunge into the deeper waters of rank douchebaggery, this is your chance. If you're a female who dates the douchebag like a pill-popping housewife guzzles martinis, then now is your opportunity.

But you must act now.

If there is any hope of recovery for either you or your 'bagged one, every step in this chapter must be completed, exactly and in sequence. If you are not 100 percent dedicated to taking the necessary steps to find redemption, you will not recover. You will be doomed to reenact the Grieco/Bleeth cycle of destruction for all of eternity.

There will be moments you'll want to give up, to throw in the towel, and chug six Rockstar Energy Drinks while grinding your genitalia into a stranger to loud Gwen Stefani hip-hop remixes.

But to give in to douche temptation after having come so far would be a profound tragedy.

Not every hottie/'baggy coupling will succeed in this de-douchification process. Many pass some of the steps, only to devolve back into ass-shaking douchitude at the first scent of a Vodka/Red Bull, cigarette smoke, and Axe Bodyspray. Don't let that be you.

You have already taken the first and most important step in purchasing this guide to recovery.

You are already on the road to a 'bag-free tomorrow.

CHAPTER 9

THE TWELVE STEPS OF DE-DOUCHIFICATION

STEP 1: ACCEPT THAT YOU OR YOUR LOVED ONE IS A 'BAG

Take a moment of contemplation.

Relax. Now breathe.

Realizing you have a problem is the first crucial step to getting rid of the douche plague and coming back to a land where hotties run free of avarice and baseball caps no longer tilt.

For that alone, you have begun to make amends to the very society you've polluted with cheap cologne and inane hip-hop dance moves for far too long. Admitting that you or your loved one is a greased-up Armani/Exchange–wearing panty turd is never an easy thing. But know that you are not alone.

Many people struggle to admit they have a douchebag problem. They lie to their friends. They claim it's a "passing phase" or they're just "experimenting." They rationalize. They justify. They refuse to admit the cold dark truth that's staring them in the face.

They can't acknowledge that they have turned toward the dark side of sleazy wrongness, toward full scrotal douchebaggery. So simply admitting you have this problem is the first, and perhaps most profound, step on the road to de-'bagging.

Congratulations! You have already completed the first step. Take a moment and appreciate it.

But celebrate quickly, 'bags, hotties, and scrotal choadmunches. Because eleven steps remain. And now it gets harder.

STEP 2: HALT THE SPECTACLE

The key to completing Step 2 lies in the shared understanding and acceptance of this basic concept: *No one wants to look at you, douche face.*

No one cares.

We're not interested in your overpriced designer silk T-shirt you bought at the Armani/Exchange store at the mall. We're not impressed by how perfectly placed the dual necklace plus dog tag lie around your neck. We're not fascinated by your "guns," your backward baseball cap, or your tweezed chin pubes. We're not impressed by your shaved chest, or how you grind your doggie 'bag into your cutie from behind on the dance floor. We don't find your gyrating hips and arms to be fascinatingly dazzling.

In short, no one gives a diarrheic ferret turd.

You are with a hot girl. That is who people want to look at.

Not you.

To complete Step 2, the douche must own up to his desire to co-opt attention away from his hottie. He must admit to the desire to foreground himself and transform his presence into an object of visual spectacle to at-

tract attention from the audience he seeks to gain cultural capital from. And that, in a nutshell, is *douche essence*.

The authentic couple complements each other. They do not create discordant visual spectacles.

This is not to say that men shouldn't want to be looked at or admired. Nor do we need to revert back to the retrograde gender stereotypes from the 1950s. The douche must learn to cease utilizing visual spectacle as the means by which he gains validation of the Self. This competition for spectacle with his hottie creates disharmony, dissonance, and, thus, douchosity.

For the 'bag, accepting this truism will require patience, understanding, and enduring relentless mocking until the following effects take hold. He stops tweezing the eyebrows. He stops applying man makeup, guyliner, and orange spray-on tan-in-a-can. He stops oiling up his chest like he's an extra in the homoerotic volleyball scene in *Top Gun*.

Only through confidence in authenticity, rather than kabuki-like performative ridiculousness, can the 'bag begin to rebuild the shattered fragments of his soul. As such, Step 2 is a conceptual step only. Hottie and pukescrote should sit down and discuss their competitive need to out-spectacle each other. These discussions need not be complex. Some can run as short as ten minutes. Others might take hours. So long as the pukescrote can admit to some variation of competitive visual spectacle with his hottie, and so long as the hottie can forgive him, then and only then, is Step 2 completed. Only when the 'bag is able to admit to his narcissism and self-body worship, and genuinely pledges to reform, can the couple safely move on to Step 3.

STEP 3: TURN DOWN THE COLLAR

In many ways, the popped collar is like the turkey temperature gauge of 'bag.

Is the collar down? Then the Turkey 'Bag ain't done. He'll try to glaze himself with additional layers of L.A. Looks gel and continue baking for another forty minutes until his chin scruff turns light-brown. This process must

stop. Therefore, Step 3 requires a full commitment to cease the douche basting once and for all.

Note that the picture accompanying Step 3 does not feature a hottie to balance out the popped-collar douchebaggery. This is because it functions as an example of the most vital part of this step. The hottie must isolate popped-collar contamination by removing herself completely from any form of cohabitation with 'bag.

She cannot return until said collar has been restored to its natural turned-down position.

Hotties must withhold all affection, conversation, shouts of "Woo!", and any form of saying hello until the 'bag has maintained a de-popped collar for at least a period of seventy-two hours straight.

Physically leaving the room is not necessary, but may be required in certain cases. Some hotties will find they need to maintain at least distant proximity to the de-popped 'bag during his period of withdrawal. Shouts of encouragement can help the douchepuddle during this process. But at no point must a hottie come within a ten-foot radius.

This period of separation may be hard. But it is essential.

Only when the 'bag has resumed fully normal collar function for at least the seventy-two hour de-popping period, can the hottie return, and the couple can continue to Step 4.

STEP 4: WASH OUT THE HAIR GEL

This step may sound easy at first. De-gelling your or your boyfriend's hair might seem a simple ten-minute process that can be performed at any bathroom shower or sink.

Not true.

Washing out the gel, aka the Douchal Purge, is not simply the removal of the cruddy remnants of two weeks' worth of dried gel crust attached to a 'bagscrote's frosted hair follicles.

A heavily gelled douche is beyond mere greasy buffoonery. He is a symphony of douchal orchestration. A cacophony of phony ca-ca. Each hair follicle must be scrubbed not only with shampoo, but also with the purest of psychological intentions: an untainted desire to reform one's 'baggy ways. To reach for the gel-free state of Hair Revelation and let the sun shine in.

Both hottie and 'bag must fully and completely de-gel as an essential part of the recovery process. Not even a "little bit to get the frizz out." Healthy couples can reintegrate basic functional hair gel down the road after this process is completed. But for now a total state of gellessness is essential.

To complete Step 4, fully and completely wash out both hott and choadpoo's hair in regular four-hour intervals. Throw away any and all hair product that may be accessible during this time.

Some couples may opt to read and/or watch TV during this time. That is acceptable. Light music can also be played—Chopin, Rachmaninoff, or anything incapable of being turned into a dance remix.

Remember, washing out the gel is about cleansing the soul. It is the purging of the pud—the sterilization of the crispy, crusty forces of greasy underbelly that keep pulling a choadwank back toward the 'bag hand gestures while head-butting the hottie in the face.

Don't slip backward. Focus. You're almost halfway home.

Wait fourteen days. Only after two solid weeks of 100 percent gel-free hair, can the hottie and her choadpud continue to Step 5.

STEP 5: LEAVE NEW JERSEY

The most direct route to leaving the state of New Jersey is, of course, via the turnpike. Which exit you take is up to you.

But do not leave immediately.

Before exiting the state, be sure to do the following:

1. Terminate or otherwise legally end your mortgage or lease.
2. Pack your clothes, furniture, and cherished heirlooms. Do not pack any hair products, body sprays, or energy drinks.
3. Notify friends and loved ones of your move. Explain why. They should

be loving and encouraging. If not, they are probably infected with the Douche Virus and can be ignored and removed from your Last Will and Testament.

4. Locate any one of a number of moving companies in New Jersey, including Hercules Movers, All American Moving and Storage, and Douche-Off Express. Consult your local Yellow Pages for more information on van rental prices.

Only when all physical and emotional ties to the region are severed, are you ready. Find the fastest and most direct route to exit the state to New York or Pennsylvania, or drown yourself in the Hudson.

While moving may feel extreme, especially for those born and raised in the Garden State, it is imperative to note that this is one of the most essential steps in the de-douchification process, because it demonstrates strength of anti-scrotal dedication. Failure to take this step betrays a lack of commitment at truly purging the grease stain within one's douched-out soul.

If you are not willing to take this step, you are not genuine in your desire for reform and repentance. Perhaps you would prefer to put down this book and return to the clubs, where skeezy, oily, Jersey douches like the one pictured here would be happy to make your or your girlfriend's acquaintance.

Alternatives to Step 5 include leaving Long Island, Miami Beach, Scottsdale, Arizona, and/or setting fire to Dallas.

STEP 6: LOSE THE BLING

Step 6, like Steps 3 and 4, appears to be simple. Unclasping your numerous faux-diamond pendants may seem easy. But it is not. This step is actually one of the most important and difficult parts of the process along the path of douchal rehabilitation.

Hotties should participate equally in this ritual, assisting and emotionally supporting their douchepuddle during his piece-by-piece removal of every level of finger, wrist, arm, and neck bling.

This includes giant glittering rapper necklaces, up to and including Jesus Bling itself, as well as all assorted trinkets like rings, belts, and earrings.

For the long-term douchestain, this step can be quite painful. Some experience deep bling withdrawal, in which 'bags feel naked, emotionally shattered, and strangely cold. Some have been known to relapse, attempting to tape paperclips to their chests and wrap aluminum foil around their wrists during detoxification.

Be ready for this.

Remove all glittery objects from the location of treatment that could possibly serve as surrogate bling. Go slowly. Wait a few hours after each specific piece of bling removal, if need be. Be sure the scrotepoo is fully ready to move on before continuing. Do not rush him.

A hottie-douchey couple should go at least five consecutive days without bling relapse before moving on to Step 7.

STEP 7: UNTILT THE HAT

Untilting the Ten-degree Hat Tilt (10DHT), like Step 6's bling removal, has emotional upheaval that far outweighs the specific acts involved in the process. The most common reflexive response from the scrotechoad is, "But [famous rapper] does it, and he looks bangin'! So why can't I?"

Because, Dr. Seussbag, the emulation of black hip-hop stars by suburban white douchebags is one of the great societal crimes of the entire 'bag plague. Modern douchebaggery is drenched in this subcultural violation.

So quit it. Unless you're a rapper, you look like a tool.

Hotties, participate in this step with your douche. Encourage him to tilt back to zero degrees. If he's struggling, allow him to move to 180-degree reverse hat tilt as a comforting intermediary step for a couple of days.

Remember, always support him, as he will appear vulnerable during this transition and often may attempt to interject as many "yo"s into the conversation as possible. Just ignore these guttural outbursts of hip-hop withdrawal as cries for help. It is merely his unease in transitioning back from suburbanite rapified überdouche to real human being.

And remember, the subtext of this step is to not simply move your already annoying baseball cap back to at least the basic position it was intended. It is to free your soul from douchey hip-hop emulation.

The couple should wait at least one full day with zero-degree Hat Tilt before moving on.

STEP 8: REMOVE THE MANDANA

The mandana (or male bandana), worn either in tandem with 10DHT or by itself, is one of the key staples of modern douchebaggery. It is the place where hip-hop meets southern rocker in a cultural clash of chaotic choad-baggery.

Even when adorned with noble motives, say, the hiding of a receding hairline or lobotomy scar, the mandana is a fundamental problem. It must be removed, deloused, and set aflame with lighter fluid.

If you're unsure about whether you're witnessing a mandana in its douche state, ask yourself if you have the following reaction: "Megods, there's enough cloth in that swath for the Italian artist Christo to wrap half of Utah with."

If so, you are in the presence of douche mandana.

Assist your 'bag by slowly and carefully untying the cloth. Reassure him. He will be vulnerable. Hide all hair gel and 10DHT for the duration of this process.

For a late-stage douchepoo, the fully exposed head feels profoundly naked and terrifying. Help him. Soothe him. Observe him through a two-way mirror in hourly intervals. While some 'bags have been known to go into a fetal position and whimper quietly, do not let this sway you to return the mandana back to him. For that is what he wants.

Simply wait it out.

Play soothing whale song recordings, or post–*Blade Runner* Vangelis. Tell him he looks fine. Usually within forty-eight hours the doucherot will begin to revive himself and ask for an ice-cream Chipwich. Reward him with a Chipwich. They're quite tasty.

Only when the de-mandanda'd choadscrote is fully secure and able to function again, without any forehead cloth to hide behind, will the couple be fully ready to move to Step 9.

STEP 9: DE-GREASE THE DOUCHE FACE

Like many variations of Douche Aura, the Douche Face presents douchosity not as commodity fetish, like hat tilt or bling, but as a psychoanalytic manifestation, or a deep-rooted projection of the Self from within.

As such, it is harder to cure than simply removing the sweat-caked remnants of, say, the hair gel cleanup in Step 4.

First, the hottie should lie her boyfriend down in a comfortable, dark place and apply pressure to his face with a moist towelette. You must wipe the grease off at regular hourly intervals for a few days straight. He may cry out for Axe Bodyspray or his desire to get another tribal tattoo.

These are simply the cries of withdrawal. Pay them no heed.

Various chemical aftershave lotions will begin to dot the forehead like so many pools of rancid oil. Be prepared for this, and continue to clean in regular intervals.

By the fifth day of this cleansing operation, the forehead should begin to recover a semblance of normalcy. At this point slowly reintroduce him to regular daylight activity. Prevent any exposure to Red Bull, *Details* magazine, or images of Ryan Seacrest for at least a month.

It is important to remember that the douche face emanates from the forehead, eyebrows, and smirky mouth like amplified radiation. As such, it will reappear randomly, seemingly without explanation. Do not be alarmed by this development. Simply continue cleaning and reassuring the scrotepud with a soothing tone of voice.

When you are convinced that the forehead is no longer producing oil at a rate that rivals Riadyh, Saudi Arabia, you are ready to move to Step 10.

STEP 10: BREAK THE DOUCHE-TO-HOTT VIRUS REPLICATION

One of the main pathways that douche current travels is through basic physical contact. The more physical contact, the more doucheyness grows.

What this means is that Douche Effect is never a locatable toxin, as it is always in motion. It is constantly fluctuating between the pumped-up schlort and the hottie who compliments and reinforces his patterned head-shaving überscrotebaggery.

Or, put another way, she says "yes" to his doucheyness and in response, he douches way harder.

To break this cycle, the circuit of douchosity reinforcement must be shut off like a spigot. This complimentary action to Step 2 means that the hottie can no longer react to the performance of the peacocking male. She must reject his 'bag overtures or risk reinforcing the paradigm.

To complete this step, the 'bag must do something utterly scrotorious in the presence of the hottie. Shave weird patterns into his hair. Pump his fists wildly to the latest tracks from Timbaland. Make the kissy lips.

The hottie must then clearly and overtly reject these overtures through distinct and unambiguous body language. She must disavow any and all physical contact until such peformative douchuousness ends.

This means no boobie grabs or sloppy makeout sessions.

This step may need to be repeated a number of times before the negative reinforcement takes effect. Like training a dog. Thus, the onus of passing Step 10 rests fully on the hottie's ability to resist and retain the 'bag's actions.

Give this step at least five days. Only when the entire five-day cycle has passed without hottie affirmation of wanky behavior in the scroadbowl, can the couple safely move to Step 11.

STEP 11: RELAX THE 'BAG HAND GESTURE

An interesting scrotological development, the origin of the 'Bag Hand Gesture remains mysterious and elusive.

Some posit it simply as a cry for attention. Others describe it as an animalistic echo, like when Balisian rhesus monkeys fling poo or Canadian chipmunks whistle various 50 Cent ringtones in the hopes of attracting a mate.

Early historiographical theory explores the notion that 'Bag Hand Gestures (#001–#265) first came into use in late nineteenth-century dance halls when dockworkers would signal to find out if a woman nearby was a lady of the evening. Throughout much of Douche Antiquity, these early proto-douche hand signs would make recurrent appearances. So they are neither new, nor unique, in their modern manifestation. But they remain as potent a signifier of douchebaggery today as when they were first introduced.

To properly complete Step 11, the presence of a digital flash camera is required.

The hottie and douchebag should position themselves in a dark, smoky room to simulate either a club or bar. Props may be used, such as lemon-drop shot glasses, ubiquitous red cups, or cans of Miller Lite. A third person may be required to operate the camera, or it can simply be set on a timer.

In advance of the actual test, douchewanks may want to practice posing on their own in front of a mirror. Relax all hand muscles. Smiling is not required, and douche face expressions must also be fully avoided. Only when the choad-scrote feels ready should you bring in the camera.

The hottie and 'bag should now position themselves in front of the camera and prepare to have their picture taken. The first instincts of the 'bag will be to raise his hand and proudly announce his greasy douchitude through a ridiculous hand gesture. Either sideways peace sign, the Shocker, or the Westside. This impulse will not be easy to overcome.

It is OK if the first few pictures snapped find the scrotepoo making 'Bag hand gestures. Do not panic. This is simply part of the process. After an inadvertent gesture, stop and breathe for sixty seconds before resuming.

Stay quiet. Stay focused. Keep trying. Do not quit.

Successful passing of this step can be measured when the hottie/douchey couple can take at least ten consecutive digital pictures without the 'bag engaging in even one mildly scrotey hand gesture.

Again, if you suffer setbacks, do not give up. You simply must focus. Eventually, you will pass this crucial step of de-douchifying de-douchification.

Once completing Step 11, both hottie and scroteblister should take the time to celebrate their accomplishments. This is a major turning point in the road to recovery. You're almost all the way there.

STEP 12: DISBAND THE WOO HOTTIES AND DOUCHE SCRUMS

This last and final step of de-douchification is one that must be undertaken by both parties. Both cutie and scrotefungus must confront, yet fully remove themselves spiritually, from the collective participation of woo hottie and douche scrum.

To take this final step to purge *The 'Bag Within* once and for all, the 'bag/hot couple must resist temptation to dive back into the swirling chaos of the name-brand collective soup and find their self-worth outside of culturally shared validation. Each must confront, and reject, the alluring pull of the noxious club group swirl. Each must find his or her authenticity. Each must stand on his or her own as individuals. Only then can they get together as a true couple.

This is not to say that the hottie/douchey couple can't find time to party with a group of friends. Step 12 resides on a deeper level of root impulse.

To pass this final test, you and your loved one must return to the club. Pick the darkest, most foul popped-collar scrotery, and enter. But do not drink.

Witness the woo hottie scrum. Witness the circling douchebags angling to grab a straying woo hottie and bump and grind her from behind in classic Doggie 'Bag position.

Now ask yourselves this: Do you feel compelled to jump into the fray? If so, can you resist?

Douchebags, do you want to smack the ass of a straying woo hottie as she passes?

Hotties, do you want to "Woo!"?

Of course you do. We all do. But can you resist? Until you pass this final step, until you can face down your douchebaguous past once and for all, you will never be sure.

The 'bag must refrain from participating in dance floor scrums of three or more woo hotties shouting "Hey!" and "Ho!" and then "Hey!" and then "Ho!" Concurrent to the 'bag's resistance, the female must also resist the urge to commingle within this larger mash-up of human flesh, sweat, large sunglasses, and designer belt buckles made of diamelles and brass.

Give yourself the entire night. Simply observe. Detach. Are you no longer dazzled by the bling? Do the facial carvings and group shoutings of performative joy strike you as silly instead of impressive? Something you no longer need or desire?

If so, if you can make it, if you can pass these twelve steps, I have one word and one word only: CONGRATULATIONS!!

You have de-Bleethed and de-Douchified and you are well on your way back to a functioning reality outside of the spectacular douchitude of our collective societal fester.

You are an individual again.

Good work! And welcome back. We've missed you.

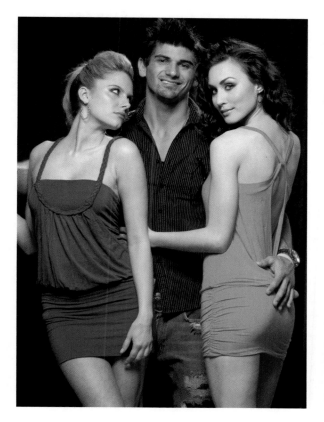

Successfully de-douched couple Tami and Anson, celebrating their one-month, douche-free anniversary by having a threesome with Tami's best friend Shelly, who's, like, totally gonna regret it tomorrow.

CHAPTER 10

HEART OF DOUCHENESS

If the radiance of a thousand suns, were to burst at once into the sky, that would be like the splendor of the Mighty Scrote . . . I am become Douche, the shatterer of Worlds.

—THE 'BAGAVAD-GITA

MY PROCESS OF classifying all the stages and permutations of douchebaggery completed, I had but one mission remaining. One final quest.

I had to confront the Source. The place where every permutation of global douchebaggery pilgrimages to visit at least once a year. For until I took this step, until I confronted the Heart of Doucheness itself, I would never be free.

I had to go to Douche Mecca.

The Hard Rock Hotel and Casino in Las Vegas, Nevada.

DOUCHE MECCA

I took my car from Los Angeles, traveling alone on Route 5. I reached the outskirts of Vegas at dusk.

I felt beads of sweat drip down the back of my neck. The sweat of anticipation. Of confrontation. Of scrotal vibration and transformation.

I pulled off the highway and turned onto the main strip, rolling down my window and taking a deep breath of the dry desert air. The sunlight was fading, and the Vegas skyline was lit up like a pinball machine.

I watched as tourists scurried like feral hamsters along the strip. Overweight, pasty Midwesterners, huffing like walruses toward the $7.99 Eat-n-Greet Buffet at the Golden Nugget, as if suburban Indianapolis had thrown up in front of my car.

But these ambulatory meatwiches were harmless. They were not the 'bags I sought.

I continued down the endless concrete river as the sky turned black. I passed Bally's. The MGM Grand. Caesar's Palace.

I arrived at my motel and pulled into the parking structure, half a mile from

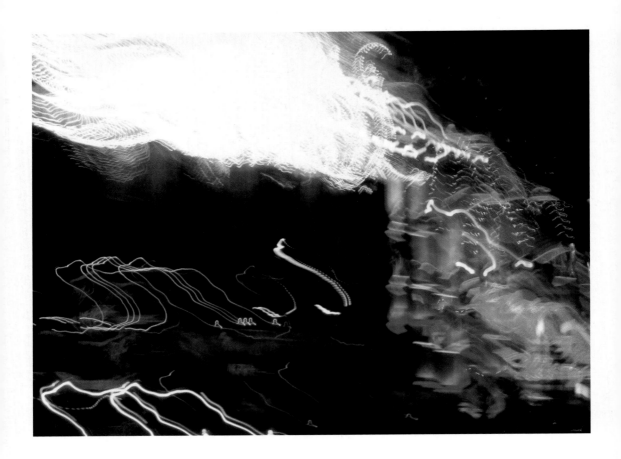

the Hard Rock Casino. Half a mile from Douche Mecca. My motel wasn't fancy, but good enough for me to rest up before continuing my journey in the morning.

I was exhausted. I checked in, went up to my room, and quickly passed out.

The next morning the motel air-conditioning blew through my room with arctic chill. I opened my eyes, climbed out of bed, and pulled open the curtains. I glanced out my motel room window into the morning light. I was far from home, in a sandy oasis gilded by the losings of many an Asian businessman.

I ate a Ho Ho.

An hour later, dressed and showered, I pulled out of the hotel parking lot in my car. I pulled off the strip and headed directly into that primitive, primal morass of carefully designed parking structures and sleazy liquor stores. There was no turning back now.

And then I saw it. The sign shimmered in the morning sunlight like a glittering dream of surreal abstraction rendered crystalline real. The Hard Rock Casino. Douche Mecca.

It was Sunday, the holiest day of douchal congregation in this, the unholiest of Scrotal Temples. On the other side of the casino's shimmering gates, by the pool area, awaited the singular most important celebration of douchebaggery/hotness commingling in all of post-Grieco society: the Rehab Ball. Like Easter, Yom Kippur, and Flag Day all rolled into one. Only with lots of hair gel and a DJ named Raccoon X.

Approach cautiously, a voice said in my head.

Who are you? I thought.

It is me, Ishmael. Talking Bottle of Vidal Sassoon Hair Gel. I'm with you.

"My name's not Ishmael!" I snapped, aloud this time.

No need to talk out loud, Ishmael. I'm with you in spirit. I'm here to help you on your final journey.

I parked in the lot and entered the casino cautiously. The large glass doors opened and I was immediately greeted by a blast of dissonant noise—a loud guitar power chord. It took a moment for my overloaded synapses to process the song, but then I recognized it.

"Come Sail Away," by Styx.

The eighties guitar-rock anthem blasted through my insides, vibrating my uvula with g-force effect. A centrifugal force that pulled on my inner scrotudinae, shattering my confidence.

I tried to control my throbbing head and raspy breathing. I was as close to the Heart of Doucheness as I'd ever imagined I'd get. I was Orpheus. I had found my flaming underworld, and it was smelly douche poo.

There was no turning back now. I forced myself to enter.

The doors closed behind me and I found myself on the main casino floor. Überbags and überhotts commingled everywhere. Muscled-up fratchoads clutching thin blue bottles of Miller Lite in one hand and young, confused doe-eyed hotties of partially revealed boobies with the other. They were transponders of sonic urscrote, crowding the card tables, clogging up the restaurants, and loitering by the twenty-five-cent video poker machines.

I approached the entrance to the pool area: the gateway itself.

A long line of aspiring douche/hott combos shuffled nervously in front of me. They emitted only faint cries of "Woo!" as they nervously waited to gain entrance to the Douchal Temple. Some applied gel reinforcements to their foreheads and frosted hair. Others tried to slyly remove the crease from their popped collar.

At the front of the line stood the ferryman. His popped-collar, spikey-haired presence was so far beyond regular douche, so far beyond überdouche, he

could spontaneously create a new element on the periodic tables—Douche Nine.

I decided that was his name. Douche Nine. A periodic element of douchosity. A primary metal of embryonic wankpuddery.

Douche Nine was the ruler of this underworld. He was the chosen one, entrusted with taking those greasy enough across the barrier and into the heart of Douche Mecca. He was the final obstacle on my path.

Stay strong, Ishmael, Talking Bottle of Vidal Sassoon Hair Gel reassured me. *Find your inner strength, and you will pass.*

I knew what I had to do.

I rushed to the nearby bar. I slapped down my money and purchased two highly overpriced cans of Miller Lite. I removed my shirt and tied it around my waist. I pulled up my hair as high as it would go.

I felt the very muscles in my face began to transform. I was making the douche face. I was becoming *The 'Bag Within*.

I maneuvered directly in front of Douche Nine's poppy spike visage. He had nowhere else for his feral gaze to dart. He sampled my 'bag essence with his highly trained eye.

A long moment passed. And then he nodded slightly, almost imperceptibly. "Let this one through!" he barked to his bouncer.

And just like that, I was in.

I walked through that spectral tunnel like a dizzy and delirious traveler on the roadway of psychosomatic transformation. Tiny animated douchepuds from my past curled up hotties in their arms and danced a conga across my synapses. I was out of mind. Between polarities. Between sanity and hair spike.

I had arrived. I blinked in the bright sunlight.

Artificial pools snaked through the palm trees like giant aqua vipers. Sun-baked walkways were covered in a sea of greased-up flesh. Writhing bodies pumped their arms to techo like a crypto-fascist orgy. Orange tanned hottie/douchey couplings dripping foul cocktails of hair gel and last night's DNA into the water like a swirling expulsion of liquid douchebaggery.

"Woos!" rang out and echoed through the cavern like siren calls of

douche legend. 'Bags and hotties gesticulated with the privileged stance of Douche Gods on the Island of Delos.

I glanced up at the DJ booth. He raised his hand in the air. Then waved it like he just didn't care.

The 'bags said "Hey." Then they said "Ho." I glanced quickly at the roof. It was not on fire.

The monotonous vibrations of techno thumped a primal rhythm. *Boom-tiss-boom-tiss-boom-tiss-boom* . . . like a mecha-robot Transformer or the Wonder Twins activating, I watched as überhott and überbag danced intricate fractal patterns in nauseating unison. Pectoral muscles flexed with the straining ligaments of dystopian hellfire.

As the throbbing rhythm increased in speed and intensity, the 'bags began to chant loudly—primal grunts of approval.

I glanced to the upper level of rock formations, where misting machines sprayed down over the cabanas. Warm chlorinated pool water mixed with cocktails and stale Old Spice to fill my nostrils with pungent dread.

They were above me. They were below me. The air grew fallow with the stench of Tag Bodyshots. My eyes clenched shut. I could hardly breathe. I was trapped.

No. You must witness.

The voice cut through the pounding techno and shook me back from the brink.

I can't!

You must open your eyes and confront Douche Mecca. Or your journey will remain incomplete. Forever.

I knew that Talking Bottle of Vidal Sassoon Hair Gel was right.

I forced my legs to start moving and pressed onward, stepping over discarded muscle shirts and pink Polo short sleeves. I headed down the bridge and toward the far side of the pool. Death Metal Rockerbags crashed into me, double-fisting Vodka and Red Bulls as they grunted approvingly at passing boobie bounces. Nearby, thirty fratpuds did a synchronized Guido Dance.

I looked down at the water. Its human fluid saturated murkiness was a sickly milky gray.

Along the riverbed shore were dozens of curvy balls of sexed up hot. Less polluted than the woo hotties, these young flowers still retained some semblance of original bloom. Their breasts shook like grapefruits filled with sand and helium.

It was for them that I journeyed. For them that I suffered under the cruel desert sun in this savage and strange land.

I locked eyes with one. She was about 5'6", wearing a bikini and large sunglasses. She smiled and gave me the thumbs up.

I felt like writing love poetry in Sanskrit to her honor and burying it for a thousand years just to confuse archaeologists. I wanted to grab her, pull

her from the clutches of the nearby scrotebags in such a way that I could cop a feel, and then run until my legs couldn't carry me any farther.

But I couldn't slow down or I would drown in the grease swirl. I had to keep moving.

I stumbled down the far side of the pool area, stopping to survey the landscape. The writhing bodies in the water began to come together like some spectral apparition of pure group-think. I stepped back, gasping.

Suddenly, I saw something, high above me, floating like a spectral burst of electric neon current.

I gazed up in awe. I held my breath and strained to make out its shape.

It was a face: *the Face of Grieco.*

Three stories high. Shimmering with ghost-like translucency.

And next to it, there she was: *the Face of Bleeth.* Pure. Innocent. Happy again.

I had come to the precipice. The cultural divide of twenty years of decay personified in this pulsing vortex: this douche abyss. Here I was, at the end of my journey.

I had traveled across the lands, classifying every permutation of douche-hott manifest. And now I had come here, to Douche Mecca, to face my deepest, darkest demons one final time.

I stared at the Faces of Grieco and Bleeth for a long moment.

And suddenly it hit me.

My collar did not have to pop. My hair could remain free of cactus spike. I need not get a Chinese

word tattooed on my abs. I didn't have to adorn myself with bling or make ridiculous shocker hand gestures. My pants could remain at waist level—my underwear unrevealed.

I thought back on my travels, everything that had led me to this point. And I thought of Lauren, my long ago ex-girlfriend, and the inspiration for my journey into the heart of doucheness.

A feeling of calm came over me. I closed my eyes. I was ready.

Good-bye, Lauren, I thought to myself.

And I knew Talking Bottle of Vidal Sassoon Hair Gel smiled.

• • •

I followed the dark murky current as it lead me out of the jungle swamp. The crowd, that rhythmic pulsing organic mass, parted in front of me as if sharing a collective conscious awareness that I was not of this land.

I reached the entrance back to the casino with a deep sense of calm. My forehead glistened with the last few beads of sweat as I pulled my shirt back on. The crashing dissonant noises of the pool woo party began to fade from my ears. I shook off the Miller Lite and salty odors that lurked within my nostrils like a funky DJ's low self-esteem lurks behind his faux-hawk.

I entered the casino and left Douche Mecca quickly, but calmly. I did not look back. I didn't need to. I had seen what I came to see. I had confronted what I had to confront. And I had said good-bye.

I was free.

THE JOURNEY HOME

An hour later I checked out of my motel room, the pungent fumes of sweat and hair gel rapidly fading from my nostrils. The cries of "Woo!" still echoing in my ears, but only distantly now.

I got in my car and pulled back onto the highway.

It was early afternoon, at least 105 degrees outside. I rolled down the window and let the crackling air blow through the car loudly.

On the outskirts of town, about forty-five minutes outside of Vegas proper, a small clump of hotels and restaurants sat off to the side of the road. I realized that I hadn't eaten since the previous night so I parked by a small local diner.

I took my seat in the brightly-lit chrome and porcelain trolley car and read the menu.

"Can I get you something?" a voice asked.

I glanced up at the waitress. She was a dusty small-town beauty. Bright-eyed, with milky skin and large breasts that jiggled like bouncy rubbery balls at the Chuck E. Cheese.

"Uhm, sure. Yeah. I'll have a coffee and the bacon and eggs, scrambled." I stuttered, dazzled by her glow.

"Sure thing! I'll be right back."

She bounded off into the kitchen and I watched her buttocks shake like a ferret with Parkinsons.

She came back with a porcelain mug and a coffeepot, and poured coffee. I studied her every detail as she did so. Her neckline. Where the top of her uniform met the nape of her pinkish upper shoulder.

When she finished she paused and glanced at me.

"Thanks," I said.

"You're welcome, sweetie!" she replied brightly. And she smiled, holding my gaze.

An open, warm smile of delight.

A pure visceral celebration of youth, vitality, and attractive fondle-worthy boobosity. Her joy at simply being alive. And her joy in seeing my pleased reaction.

In that instant, something clicked. Something I hadn't found back at Douche Mecca. In that moment, in the eyes of a young innocent beauty working a crap job on the outskirts of town, I saw something special: the flash of genuine understanding.

The universe cracked its eggshell, opened up its secrets, and offered a bright angelic light of hope, pouring forth over me like strands of golden pollen. Within her gaze, within the extra half-second or so that she held my eyes, there was an instantaneous spark of mutual recognition—of connection.

All that affected performativity melted away in a blur of out-of-focus swirling Armani/Exchange T-shirts and 10DHT. All that cultural chaos was flushed away like so much detritus. Tossed aside like fallow rotting driftwood. Yesterday's gel. Last week's brand name.

Instead of confusing each other with the armor of performance, there was a flash of nonverbal mutual understanding. A connection across that expansive divide that so often seems insurmountable.

What remained were just two people. Sharing a moment over watered-down coffee poured into a porcelain mug sitting on a Formica countertop in rural Nevada. No name-brand validation needed. No glossy dress-up. No hand gestures, hair gel, or bling. I didn't need to prove my merit by clutching a giant bottle of Grey Goose vodka. She felt no need to let loose with cries of "Woo!"

I had stared down the überbags at the Hard Rock. I had looked back at Douche Antiquity, traced the virus all the way through the Grieco and into the modern day. But even after I'd immersed myself within a media culture saturated by designer label object, fetishized style, and trendy collective culture stampede, authenticity remained.

I simply had to find it.

I finished my coffee and paid the bill. I got back in my car and left.

I made it home in less than three hours.

RICHARD GRIECO PASSES ON THIS

Date Tue, 25 Sep
"Jay Louis" <jaylouis@xxxxxx.com>
To: "Tracy Q." <txxxx@xxxxxx.com
Subject Re: Richard Grieco

Tracy—
I still haven't heard from you on whether or not Richard is willing to write the afterward to my book 'Hot Chicks with Douchebags.' I hope he'll consider it, as having someone so historically important to the history of douchebag-gery would be a huge honor. Any thoughts?
Sincerely,
Jay Louis,
Writer Hot Chicks with Douchebags
Los Angeles, CA

Date Tue, 25 Sep
"Tracy Q." <txxxx@xxxxxx.com>
To "Jay Louis" <jaylouis@xxxxxx.com>
Subject Re: Richard Grieco

Sorry for the delay . . . Thank you for thinking of Richard; unfortunately, he is going to pass on this . . . we wish you all the best . . . truly, we do!!!
Regards,
Tracy Q.
H_____ Entertainment
Encino, CA

ACKNOWLEDGMENTS:
SPECIAL THANKS

THIS BOOK is based on my blog www.hotchickswithdouchebags.com. I started it in March of 2006[1] after a night of excess drinking and inchoate rage at witnessing the hottie/douchey phenomenon firsthand on the streets of Los Angeles. I must give a special round of thanks to all the participants and contributors on the blog whose enthusiasm and hilarious commentary mocking the douchescrote and celebrating the hott have kept me going.

To Mark Pfahlert for his brilliant Photoshop work on the pics in Chapter 4, a hearty 'Bag Hunter of the Year award. To Rea-Silvia Feriozzi for her wonderful Darwin Douche Penguins sketch, you've supported my creative endeavors for many a moon with no more financial compensation than a hearty handshake. You and Jim will always be my favorite married couple of non-douchebaggery. And to excellent 'bag hunters Ryan Powles and Matt Jacobs, you have been invaluable members of the community from the beginning and help me keep the site poppin' fresh on a daily basis.

Some of the regulars on the website that I'd like to thank include, in no particular order:

greekbag, baron von douchehausen, voodouche child (slight return), baron von goolo, blinded by the light dressed up like a douche, doc, lower

---

[1]*Hot Chicks with Douchebags* receives approximately 600,000 unique visitors and more than 1,500,000 page views a month, based on May 2008 Google Analytics.

case bag, darksock, bmt, lemon tart, doucheburglar, douchetorious b.a.g., douchebag out!, kellybelly, Mistress Julie, Ian, ron douchegay, mctickle, George W. Douche, father guido sardouchey, b.a. douche, pfah, ibling, the 'baggernaut, rebel without a douche, bk, diego, skanderbag, anthony labaglia, maximum overdouche, douche mcallister, danny bonnadouchey, nick, scrotebob douchepants, bcs, nostradouchemas, douche bagwell, danny noonan, shadowspawn, norse douche destroyer, eric cartman, HanksAnAss, bursny, scrunt, plinky, moondancer, douche vader, deloitte and douche, john edwards, reservoir douche, Don Juan de la Douche, admiral hamilton mantitty, lindsey douchehan, rubber douchey, Johnny bravo, bag em dano, thin white douche, BAGwan Singh, rip van wanker, el douchablo, Celeb Douche, Lighter Shade of Douche, sadbag, sleeperbag, snoop douchey douche, el doucherino if you're not into the whole brevity thing, the douche is loose, beauty and the douche, douche springsteen, count douchula, Clementine of Cappadoucha, motherofsquirrelkiller, jailergrrl, the bag apple, bub, haagen douche, honus bagner, ed, the douchess of kunt, maximus, ol' dirty douchebag, never_a_bag, maximum overdouche, perez douche, boatbutter, hott_tron 3000, army of Doucheness, mitch meats, scroto baggins, sir Douche-a lot, The Arch Douche, marcos douchbagdatis, Otto Graf von Douchemark, cleavite stalagmite, cc, newman's own balsamic douche, ron douchegay, spinnaker chick, 23 Skidouche, the douche the douche the douche is on fire, gunna, mr. white, scroter the unstoppable douche machine, Bill Bellidouchechick, snoop douchey dog, t.j. douchemandzadeh, douchelicious, xander dingleberries, arch 'bagger of canturbury, jeff bagwell, Ryan Seadouche, vacuum cleaner bag, dion didouchie, batou, stuporfly, the stink, creature, sir robert muldouche, ron tugnut, jonezy, mytaint, ted Theodore scrotgan, the big douchebagski, no country for old douchebags, douche cousteau, douche gently, poo convention, and you will know us by the trail of douche, x, indiana douche, douchey howser m.d., 'bagamemnon, il choadrino, kofi anonymous, to douche or not to douche, replicantx, squatch, chodewart, duke of douchester, douche willis, jack nickelbag, dildo baggins, 'Bagavad Gita, lone scrote mcquade, sleeperbag, bagglio ordonez, bagwagger, eradicooter, don parmesan guido linguini, turner and douche, dita von douche, douche against the machine, greekbag, 'bag hater, scroteface killah, notadouche, the hate crime, celeb douche, i bling, boingy, douchebagger vance, Rage Against the Douchine, where's waldouche?, doucheacabra, douchevid hasselhoff, Scooby doobie douche, k-federbag, douchestar runner and, of course, *the ever present anonymous.*

If I left anyone off the list, it is only because I am an alcoholic douche-wank. Their brilliant and inspired comments helped push me to probe deeper into the cultural trainwreck of our MySpace- and Facebook-infested exhibitionist scrotey collective societal trauma. And if you think that's a run-on sentence, you should see my other car.

Without their participation and encouragement, this book would never have been possible. Which may or may not be a good thing.

Special thanks to Alex Frangos, David Vigliano, Michael Harriot, Kirby Kim, Luis Kain, Anson Avellar, my editor Ursula Cary, and Jeremie Ruby-Strauss for believing in the power of the scrote when it was just my silly rantings on a far-off corner of the worldwide Interwebs.

And finally I must give thanks to anyone and everyone who has ever found themselves or their loved ones featured in an HCwDB pic, on either the blog or here in the book. Without you I'd be deconstructing my own douchebaggery on a daily basis. Which is a scary thing.

In short, I'm in therapy.

APPENDIX:

GLOSSARY OF TERMS

To facilitate the ease of your trip into the hottie/douchey plague, I've included this detailed glossary of terms. If, during this book, you hit an expression that you don't understand, simply refer to this section for clarification. If you can't find the word in this section, that probably means you're drunk. Stop drinking. Your friends hate you.

Adouchrements. The various items a 'Bag wears to proclaim the Douche State has been achieved. See also *bling*.

Autodouche. Any specific act, gesture, or product so douchebaggy that it immediately quantifies a person as 'bag.

Babagadouche. Any sleazy Middle Eastern, Northern African, or Minnesotan douchebag.

'Bag. Short for *douchebag*.

'Bagamemnon. A commander of the Greek Douche Army during the Trojan condom wars during pledge week.

'Bag hand gesture (#01–#227). The arsenal of hand gestures made by a douchebag upon corralling a hottie for a pic. Favorites include the sideways peace sign (#36), the *West Side* (#14), and the highly popular *Shocker* (#159).

'Baggle royale. Any situation in which two or more douchebags are vying for douche supremacy through direct competition.

'Bagling. A young, budding douchebag, usually under the age of eighteen.

'Bagological development. Tracking douche evolution across a number of generations.

'Bag patch. A small fungus looking patch of facial hair on the lower part of the face. See also *Facial pubes.*

'Bag hunting. The goal of snapping a picture of a douchebag with a hot chick in their natural habitat.

'Bag sandwich formation. Two überdouches crushing a hottie between their musky grease when posing for a picture. See also *Inverted 'bag sandwich formation.*

'Bagstock. Any festival event featuring at least ten douchebags within spitting distance of one another. Sometimes referred to as a *Douche Minyan.*

Beelzebag. A douchebag whose existence is Satanic in nature.

Bleeth. Any former hottie turned female douchebag. Refers to what happened to *Baywatch* actress Yasmine Bleeth after dating actor Richard Grieco (aka Prince Grieco, aka the Holy Source Douche, aka the Grieco Virus) and other douches in the mid-1990s.

Bling. Gaudy jewelry worn by douchebags in an attempt to co-opt the gangsta rap aesthetic.

Cactus 'Bag. Any douchebag featuring gelled-up spiky hair that resembles a cactus.

Chin pubes. See also *Facial pubes.* Or better yet, don't. They're disgusting.

Choad (Chode). An out-of-shape, usually puffy-looking douchebag. A choad deviates from a standard douche when the desire to kick him in the groin provokes an involuntary muscle spasm in the knee.

Cleavite. The pale, less tanned area of the female bosom that often peeks out from behind a revealing piece of clothing. Not to be confused with *cleavage.* Although cleavage can feature cleavite, cleavite can occur on any part of the bosom, including the upper, lower, and outer rim of that soft, pillowy goodness.

Collateral douchage. Ancillary douche signifiers appearing on others in the vicinity of a primary 'bag.

Danny Bonadouchey. A red-haired clown who was once mildly famous.

Doggie 'bag. A position in which a douchebag attempts to dry-hump a hottie from behind to assert his dominance over other males in the herd.

Douche Antiquity. The historical period before 1990, also referred to as B.G. (Before Grieco).

Douchebag (aka Douche, aka 'Bag). A heterosexual male attempting to attract a mate through the use of excessive products, gels, colognes, and general sleazy demeanor. Alternate forms include *douchebaggery, douchebaguous, douchebagalicious*, and *total freaking assface*.

Douche Face. A distinctly annoying facial expression, usually found on an otherwise normal-looking dude, that instantly qualifies him for 'bag status.

Douche Mecca. The Hard Rock Hotel and Casino in Las Vegas, Nevada.

Douche Modernity. The historical period after 1990, also referred to as A.G. (After Grieco).

Douche Nirvana. New Jersey. Alternate definitions include Miami Beach, Long Island.

Douchepocalypse. A hypothetical future event when douchebaggery destroys all recorded civilization in a giant cloud of Axe Bodyspray.

Douchestrology. The mystical study of douchebaggery in an attempt to predict future events. See also *Scrotology*.

Douchezetta stone. Any photograph that offers so many decipherable clues toward understanding hottie/douchey wrongness that it holds value to future douche archaeologists.

Douchulacrum. The cultural state at which douche meaning is privileged. through visual spectacle and mediated through a form of technology. See also *Jean Doucherillard*.

Emobag. Any standard douchebag who uses stylized "sensitive" codes: dark clothes, makeup, pouty expression, etc., to convince a hottie he's "not like the others" in the hopes of getting some ass.

Facial pubes. Bizarre facial hair patterns on a 'bag that resemble a porn star's crotch. See also *Fungle.*

Faux-hawks. The whipped-up, spiky, pretend Mohawk hairstyle that is a key signifier of the presence of a 'bag.

Forehead grease. The rank, shiny substance that develops on the average 'bag's forehead during his pursuit of the female.

Fratbag. A college-age fraternity douchebag.

Fungle. Facial stubble that resembles pollen-based tree fungus.

Grieco Virus. Refers to actor Richard Grieco, the Source Douche, from whom all of modern douchebaggery has sprung.

Grillz. Removable teeth bling that appear as a diamond-studded retainer. Often worn by wigga 'bags attempting to impersonate hip-hop impresarios.

Hippiebag. Any sleazy douchebag attempting to dress like a hippie to con Wesleyan girls into stripping down while listening to Phish.

Hipsterbag. Urban indie rock–listening, frosted-haired douchebags. A variant of the Emobag.

Hot. See *Hott.*

Hott. See *Hot.*

Hottie. A young female with healthy mammaries, succulent abs, a perky nose, and a viable womb.

Inverted 'bag sandwich formation. Two hotties on either side of a douchebag, sandwiching him

Jean Doucherillard. A French philosopher of douchebaggery who did not exist.

Jelly Babies. Soft, bouncy hotties. Also, a tasty British candy favored by Doctor Who.

Jesus Bling. A large glittery fake-diamond cross, usually worn around the neck.

Kabagllah. A mystical sect that branched away from traditional douchebaggery in the eleventh century.

Kissy lips. One of the most common manifestations of the douche face, when a 'bag makes a ridiculous pout. See also *Douche Face.*

Mandana. A man's large bandana, usually found on Rockerbags.

Mark of the Douche. When the reflection in the forehead grease of a 'bag resembles male genitalia.

Moses Bling. The Jewish version of Jesus Bling, usually involving a giant glittery Star of David.

Muffin-Top 'Bag. A douche-hair look in which hair is grown out long and combed forward to create a muffin look. Mostly seen in 'baglings and high school choadlings.

Mulletbag. A noxious early 1990s strain of the Redneckbag.

Night Train. A cheap wine with high alcoholic content sold in disreputable liquor stores and favored by the author. Usually accompanied by Ho Hos or other tasty Hostess snack cakes.

Oblique Douche Factor (ODF). Subtle signs of douchebaggery that may not be apparent upon first appraisal.

PooBag. A douchebag who is so douchey that he evokes dog feces.

Popped Collar. An early warning sign of choadbaggery when an aspiring 'bag folds his collar up, creating a conical prism effect that highlights his douche face.

Portman, Natalie. Come to me, my Semitic future ex-wife. Love me. Love me forever.

Pud. Refers to a harmless or generally unthreatening douchebag, usually in his late teens.

Rastabaggian. A dirty, white, dreadlocked douchebag using unwashed hippie effect to try to corral a hottie.

Scroad. Half scrote, half choad, a squishy ball of rank douchebaggery.

Scroadbag. A douchebag who is scrotebag, douchechoad, and wankdouche, but not choadpud.

Scrote. Any douchebag who presents himself in a way that announces his "maleness" inappropriately.

Scrotebag. A douchebag who is both scroadwank, scrotechoad, and wankbag, but not choadwank.

Scrotewank. A douchebag who is wankdouche, scroatpud, überbag, and chowderpud, but not douchescrote.

Scrotifact. Evidence of previous douchebaggery.

Scrotographer. An amateur photographer skilled at capturing hottie/scrotey action pics in their natural habitat.

Scrotology. An ancient and mystical system of predicting future events based on the readings of scrotebag and hottie permutations, as well as a belief in Xenu, the ancient alien warlord who brought douchebaggery to Earth.

Source Douche. Anyone who is a primal nexus point for the creation of douche meaning.

Ten-degree Hat Tilt. The preferred positioning of a baseball cap upon one's head, usually a designer Yankees cap, to signify the presence of Douche Virus in the wearer.

Toadbag. A douchebag of reptilian appearance.

Überbag. A douchebag who transcends the bounds of mere mortal douchebaggery by moving beyond goodbaggery and evilbaggery.

Überdouchosity. A state of overwhelming douchebaggery.

Überscroadbags. See also *douchebag*.

Überscrotebags. See also *überscroadbags*.

Ubiquitous red cup. The large red plastic cups used for drinks at parties which often make appearances in the backgrounds of hottie/douche pictures.

Wank. Short for "wanker," a frustrating, aspiring douchebag who likely pleasures himself with disturbing frequency.

Wigga 'Bag. A white suburbanite appropriating black and hip-hop cultural dress.

Woogasm. A state of ecstasy reached by three or more woo hotties on the dance floor, at which point the roof is officially on fire.

Woo hotties. Three or more young women expressing simultaneous excitement and joy with a chorus of "Woo!!" Usually accompanied by raising one or two hands in the air and waving them like they just don't care.

PHOTO CREDITS